A Murder Is Announced

AGATHA CHRISTIE

Level 5

Retold by Anne Collins
Series Editors: Andy Hopkins and Jocelyn Potter

Pearson Education Limited
Edinburgh Gate, Harlow,
Essex CM20 2JE, England
and Associated Companies throughout the world.

ISBN: 978-1-4082-2112-9

This edition first published by Pearson Education Ltd 2011

3 5 7 9 10 8 6 4

Illustrations by Martin Hargreaves

Set in 11/14pt Bembo
Printed in China
SWTC/03

Published by Pearson Education Limited in association with
Penguin Books Ltd, and both companies being subsidiaries of Pearson PLC

For a complete list of the titles available in the Penguin Readers series please write to your local
Pearson Longman office or to: Penguin Readers Marketing Department, Pearson Education,
Edinburgh Gate, Harlow, Essex CM20 2JE, England.

Contents

Introduction

A murder is announced and will take place on Friday, October 29th, at Little Paddocks at 6.30 p.m. Friends, please accept this, the only notice.

It is extremely unusual for a murderer to announce the time and place of his or her crime, and to invite guests to witness it! But this is exactly what happens in *A Murder Is Announced*. The villagers of Chipping Cleghorn, an ordinary little English village, are most surprised to read in their local paper a mysterious invitation to a murder at one of their neighbours' houses. Is it a joke? Or a kind of game? They are very curious to find out, and arrive at the house at the stated time. The lights go out, a man bursts into the room and fires three shots … Fortunately, Miss Marple is staying in the area and is delighted to become involved. Miss Marple, one of Agatha Christie's most famous characters, has a deep interest in human nature which has led to the solving of a number of mysterious deaths in the past.

Born in the town of Torquay in the south of England on 15th September 1890, Dame★ Agatha Christie was the leading British writer of murder mysteries during her lifetime, and her stories have continued to be popular since her death in 1976. Her books have been translated into more than forty-five languages, and her play, *The Mousetrap*, has been on the stage in London for more than fifty years. So what made the 'Queen of Crime' such an enormously successful writer?

As a child, Agatha was educated at home, where she was allowed to choose her own books and form her own ideas. At the age of sixteen, she went to her first formal school in Paris to complete her education. Although Agatha had not planned

★ Dame: a title given to a woman as a special honour for her work to be a writer, by the time she was eleven years old one of her poems had already appeared in a local newspaper. Before she was twenty, several more of her poems had appeared in *The Poetry Review* and she had written a number of short stories.

In 1914, at the start of the First World War, Agatha married Colonel Archibald Christie. She worked in a hospital during the war, and from this experience she gained a wide knowledge of medicine and poisons. This knowledge proved very useful when she started writing detective stories: forty-one of her novels and twenty-four short stories contain murder by poison. At about the same time as the Christies' only daughter, Rosalind, was born in 1919, Agatha's sister Madge encouraged her to begin a serious writing career and write a mystery novel.

The young writer decided that she needed a detective. At the time, her home town was full of former First World War officers and soldiers who had been forced to leave Belgium. Agatha decided that one of them would make the perfect model for her famous detective, Hercule Poirot. He starred in her first detective novel, *The Mysterious Affair at Styles*, and later became the central character in thirty-three novels and fifty-four short stories.

Agatha's other famous detective creation is Miss Marple, who she based partly on her own grandmother. She did not plan to put Miss Marple into more than one book, but the public loved her so much that she eventually appeared in twelve crime novels and twenty short stories. Miss Marple looks like a sweet old lady, and enjoys ordinary activities in her small village of St Mary Mead, like gardening and having tea with her friends. But Miss Marple also has a sharp mind and an excellent understanding of human nature. She can often solve difficult crimes by comparing criminal behaviour with the behaviour of people in her village.

Agatha Christie wrote no fewer than sixty-six murder mystery novels, several plays in addition to the record-breaking *The Mousetrap*, and six romantic novels using the name Mary

Westmacott. Her extraordinary success was the result of a simple method: Agatha wrote about the world she knew, noticing every detail about real, ordinary people and places. An idea for a new story could come into her head when she was having a walk or shopping for a new hat; she filled piles of notebooks with ideas for stories and characters. She was, as her grandson Mathew Prichard has described her, '… a person who listened more than she talked, who saw more than she was seen.'

Agatha Christie's other great interests were the Middle East and travel. She met her second husband, Max Mallowan, in the Middle East in the 1930s. She loved the desert, where she and Max studied the lives of ancient peoples. She helped with these explorations and also used the places in some of her favourite books, like *Death on the Nile*, *Murder in Mesopotamia* and *They Came to Baghdad*. Towards the end of their careers, both Agatha and Max were honoured by the British government for their work. Agatha became a Dame in 1971. The nation was grateful for her entertaining stories, and she had helped to define the English way of life and character for the rest of the world.

As with all Agatha Christie's detective novels, many clues are given through the story of A *Murder is Announced*. But a reader has to be very clever in separating the real clues from the confusing false ones. The story includes everything that her admirers enjoy most: murder, a group of interesting characters, and a surprising but satisfactory solution by Miss Marple.

It is easy to understand why Agatha Christie's detective novels continue to entertain millions of readers around the world. The popularity of her stories also goes beyond the printed page. There have been many television and film productions of her mysteries, including *A Murder Is Announced*, and there are video games too. Doubtless Agatha Christie's work will continue to excite readers and audiences for many years to come.

'Isn't it wonderful?' said a female voice. 'I'm so excited!'

Chapter 1 An Extraordinary Announcement

Every morning between 7.30 and 8.30 Johnnie Butt, the newspaper boy, rode around the small village of Chipping Cleghorn on his bicycle. He stopped at each house and pushed the morning papers through the letterbox. On Friday mornings Johnnie also delivered to most of the houses a copy of the local paper, the *Chipping Cleghorn Gazette* – known simply as the *Gazette*. After a quick look at the headlines in the national papers, most people eagerly opened the *Gazette*. They glanced quickly through the Letters page, and then nine out of ten readers turned to the Personal Column.

This contained advertisements from people wanting to buy or sell things, from hens to garden equipment, or looking for help in the home. The notices in the Personal Column always interested the people of Chipping Cleghorn, but on one particular Friday – October 29th – a notice appeared which was more interesting than any of the others.

♦

Mrs Swettenham opened *The Times*, glanced through it quickly, then picked up the *Gazette*. When her son Edmund entered the room a moment later, she was busy reading the Personal Column.

'Good morning, dear,' said Mrs Swettenham. 'The Smedleys are selling their car.'

Edmund did not reply. He poured himself a cup of coffee and sat down at the breakfast table, then opened the *Daily Worker*★.

'Selina Lawrence is advertising for a cook again,' Mrs Swettenham said. 'Yes, Mrs Finch?'

The door had opened and the unsmiling face of Mrs

★ the *Daily Worker*: a newspaper with socialist political views

1

Swettenham's housekeeper appeared round it.

'Good morning, madam,' she said. 'Can I clear the table?'

'Not yet. We haven't finished,' said Mrs Swettenham.

Mrs Finch stared coldly at Edmund before leaving again.

'Why do you have to read that awful paper, Edmund?' said his mother. 'Mrs Finch doesn't like it at all.'

'I don't think my political views are Mrs Finch's business.'

'And you're not even a worker.'

'That's not true!' said Edmund. 'I'm writing a book.'

'I meant *real* work,' said Mrs Swettenham. She continued reading the Personal Column. '*A marriage is announced* – no, a *murder. What?* Edmund, listen to this … *A murder is announced and will take place on Friday, October 29th, at Little Paddocks at 6.30 p.m. Friends, please accept this, the only notice.* What an extraordinary thing! *Edmund!*'

'What's that?' Edmund looked up from his newspaper.

'Friday, October 29th … But that's today.'

'Let me see.' Edmund took the paper from his mother.

'What does it mean?' asked Mrs Swettenham.

Edmund rubbed his nose doubtfully. 'Some sort of party, I suppose. The Murder Game – that kind of thing.'

'Oh,' said Mrs Swettenham doubtfully. 'It seems a very strange way of announcing a game. It's not like Letitia Blacklock at all. She always seems to me such a sensible woman. A murder game … It sounds quite exciting.'

'It will probably be very boring. *I'm* not going,' said Edmund.

'Nonsense, Edmund,' said Mrs Swettenham firmly. '*I'm* going and *you're* coming with me.'

♦

'Archie,' said Mrs Easterbrook to her husband, 'listen to *this*.'

Colonel Easterbrook paid no attention. He was busy reading *The Times*.

'These reporters know nothing about India,' he said. 'Nothing!

If they did, they wouldn't write such rubbish.'

'Yes, I know,' said his wife. 'Archie, do listen. *A murder is announced and will take place on Friday, October 29th, at Little Paddocks at 6.30 p.m. Friends, please accept this, the only notice.*'

She paused. Colonel Easterbrook smiled at her affectionately.

'It's the Murder Game,' he said. 'That's all. One person's the murderer, but nobody knows who. The lights go out. The murderer chooses the person he's going to murder. This person has to count to twenty before he screams. Then the person who's been chosen to be the detective questions everybody. It's a good game – if the detective knows something about police work.'

'Like you, Archie. You had to deal with all those interesting cases in India. Why didn't Miss Blacklock ask you to help her organise the game?'

'Oh, well, she's got that young nephew staying with her,' said Colonel Easterbrook. 'I expect this is *his* idea.'

'It was in the Personal Column. I suppose it *is* an invitation?'

'Strange kind of invitation. *I'm* not going.'

'Oh, but Archie,' said his wife, 'I really do think you ought to go – just to help Miss Blacklock. I'm sure she's depending on you to make the game a success. One must be a good neighbour.'

Mrs Easterbrook put her blonde head on one side and opened her blue eyes very wide. Colonel Easterbrook twisted his grey moustache, and looked at his wife. Mrs Easterbrook was at least thirty years younger than her husband.

'Of course, if that's what you think, Laura …' he said.

'I really do think it's your *duty*, Archie,' said Mrs Easterbrook

♦

The *Chipping Cleghorn Gazette* had also been delivered to Boulders, the pretty cottage where Miss Hinchcliffe and Miss Murgatroyd lived. Miss Murgatroyd, a round, pleasant woman with untidy grey hair, walked through the long wet grass to the henhouse, carrying a copy of the paper.

Her friend, who had short hair and was dressed in men's workclothes, looked up from feeding the chickens.

'What is it, Amy?'

'Listen to this,' said Miss Murgatroyd. 'What can it mean? *A murder is announced and will take place on Friday, October 29th, at Little Paddocks at 6.30 p.m. Friends, please accept this, the only notice.*'

She paused, and waited for her friend to give her opinion.

'It's silly,' said Miss Hinchcliffe.

'Yes, but what do you think it means? Is it a sort of invitation?'

'We'll find out when we get there,' said Miss Hinchcliffe.

'It's a strange way to invite people, isn't it?'

But Miss Hinchcliffe wasn't listening. She was busy trying to catch a hen which had escaped.

♦

'Ooh, excellent!' said Mrs Harmon across the breakfast table to her husband, the Reverend Julian Harmon. 'There's going to be a murder at Miss Blacklock's.'

'A murder?' said her husband, slightly surprised. 'When?'

'This evening. 6.30. Oh, what a pity, darling, you won't be able to come. You've got to write your speech for tomorrow.'

Mrs Harmon, whose real name was Diana but who was usually called 'Bunch', handed her husband the *Gazette* across the table.

'There. It's among the notices in the Personal Column.'

'What an extraordinary announcement!' said her husband.

'Isn't it?' said Bunch happily. 'I suppose the young Simmonses have given Miss Blacklock the idea. I do think, darling, it's a *pity* you can't be there. I don't like games that happen in the dark. If someone touches my shoulder and whispers "You're dead", the shock might really kill me. Do you think that's likely?'

'No, Bunch,' replied her husband. 'I think you're going to live to be an old, old woman – with me.'

'And die on the same day and be buried in the same grave. That would be lovely.'

'You seem very happy, Bunch,' said her husband.

'Who wouldn't be happy if they were me?' said Bunch.

♦

At Little Paddocks, Miss Blacklock, the owner of the house, sat at the head of the table. She was about sixty years old and with her heavy country suit was wearing, rather strangely, a choker of large false pearls. Also at the table, reading the national newspapers, were her young cousins, Julia and Patrick Simmons. The fourth person at the table was Miss Dora Bunner, who was reading the local paper.

Suddenly Miss Bunner gave a cry of surprise. 'Letty – *Letty* – have you seen this? What can it mean?'

'What's the matter, Dora?' asked Miss Blacklock.

'The most extraordinary advertisement. It says Little Paddocks very clearly. But what can it mean?'

'If you'd let me see, Dora dear – ' Miss Blacklock held out her hand and Miss Bunner obediently gave her the newspaper. Miss Blacklock looked. She glanced quickly round the table. Then she read the advertisement out loud.

'*A murder is announced and will take place on Friday, October 29th, at Little Paddocks at 6.30 p.m. Friends, please accept this, the only notice.* Patrick, is this your idea?' She looked at the handsome face of the young man at the other end of the table.

'No, Aunt Letty. Why should I know anything about it?'

'I thought it might be your idea of a joke. Julia?'

Julia, looking bored, said, 'Of course not.'

Miss Bunner looked at the empty place at the table. 'Do you think Mrs Haymes –?' she said.

'Oh, I don't think Phillipa would try and be funny,' said Patrick. 'She's a serious girl.'

'But what does it mean?' said Julia, with no real interest.

Miss Blacklock said slowly, 'I suppose – it's a silly joke.'

'But why?' said Dora Bunner. 'It seems very stupid to me.'

Miss Blacklock smiled at her. 'Don't upset yourself, Bunny,' she said. 'It's just somebody's sense of humour.'

'It says today,' said Miss Bunner. 'Today at 6.30 p.m. What do you think's going to happen?'

'*Death!*' said Patrick in a low, serious voice. 'Delicious Death.'

Miss Bunner gave a little scream.

'I only meant that special cake that Mitzi makes,' said Patrick apologetically. 'You know we always call it Delicious Death.'

Miss Blacklock smiled. 'I know one thing that will happen at 6.30,' she said cheerfully. 'Half the people in the village will be here, wondering what's going to happen. I'd better make sure we've got some sherry in the house.'

♦

'You *are* worried, aren't you, Lotty?'

Miss Blacklock looked up from her writing at the anxious face of her old friend Dora Bunner. She was not quite sure what to say to her. Dora, she knew, mustn't be worried or upset. At school Dora had been a pretty, fair-haired, blue-eyed, rather stupid girl. She would surely marry a nice army officer or country lawyer. But life had been unkind to Dora. She hadn't married, but had had to work.

The two friends had lost contact. But about six months ago, Miss Blacklock had received a letter from Dora. In the letter, Dora said she was unwell. She was living in one room, with very little money. She wondered if her old schoolfriend could help.

Miss Blacklock had brought Dora to live at Little Paddocks. She had told Dora that she needed someone to help her run the house. This wasn't true, but Miss Blacklock knew that the arrangement would not be for long – Dora's doctor had told her that. Sometimes Miss Blacklock found Dora annoying. She lost bills and letters, and upset Mitzi, Miss Blacklock's foreign 'help'.

'Worried?' Miss Blacklock said eventually. 'No, not exactly. You mean, about that silly notice in the *Gazette*?'

'Yes − even if it's a joke, it seems to me it's − it's not a nice kind of joke. It frightens me. It's *dangerous*. I'm sure it is.'

The door opened and a young woman came in. Her eyes were dark and flashing.

'I can speak to you? Yes, please, no?'

Miss Blacklock sighed. 'Of course, Mitzi, what is it?'

'I am going − I am going at once! I do not wish to die. My family − they died − my mother, my little brother, my sweet little niece. But me, I ran away. I came to England. I do work that I would never − never do in my own country. I −'

'I know all that,' said Miss Blacklock. She had heard it many times before. 'But why do you want to leave *now*?'

'Because again they have come to kill me! My enemies. The Nazis*! They know I am here. They will come to kill me. It is in the newspaper!' Mitzi brought out a copy of the *Gazette* which she had been hiding behind her back. 'See − here it says a *murder*. This evening at 6.30. I do not want to be murdered − *no*.'

'But why should this be about you?' said Miss Blacklock. 'It's − we think it's a joke. If anyone wanted to murder you, they wouldn't advertise the fact in the paper, would they?'

'You do not think they would?' said Mitzi. 'Perhaps it is you who they mean to murder, Miss Blacklock.'

'I certainly can't believe anyone wants to murder me,' said Miss Blacklock lightly. 'And really, Mitzi, I don't see why anyone should want to murder *you*. We'll have beef for lunch today,' she continued. 'And some people may come for drinks this evening. Could you make some cheese snacks?'

'This evening? But who will come then? *Why* will they come?'

★ Nazis: a political group led by Adolf Hitler from 1933–1945, responsible for many deaths

7

'They're coming to the funeral,' said Miss Blacklock with a smile. 'Now, Mitzi, I'm busy.'

Mitzi went out, looking puzzled.

'You're so efficient, Letty,' said Miss Bunner admiringly.

Chapter 2   At 6.30 p.m.

'Well, everything's ready,' said Miss Blacklock. She looked around the sitting-room, checking that everything was in place. There were two bowls of roses, a small vase of violets and a silver cigarette-box on a table by the wall. Drinks had been set out on the table in the centre.

Little Paddocks was a medium-sized house built in the early Victorian⋆ style. The sitting-room had once consisted of two rooms connected by double doors. One room had been long, narrow and dark, while the other was smaller with a large window. Later, the double doors had been removed so that the two rooms became one room. There were two fireplaces, one at each end. Although neither fire was lit, the room was filled with a soft, gentle warmth.

'You've had the central heating lit,' said Patrick.

'Yes,' said Miss Blacklock. 'The weather's been so wet. The whole house felt cold.'

The door opened and Phillipa Haymes came in. She was tall and fair with a calm appearance.

'Hello,' she said in surprise. 'Is it a party? Nobody told me.'

'Of course,' said Patrick. 'Our Phillipa must be the only woman in Chipping Cleghorn who doesn't know.' He waved his hand around like an actor on a stage. 'Here you see the scene of a murder!' He pointed at the bowls of flowers. 'Those are the

⋆ Victorian: relating to the time when Victoria was queen of England, from 1837–1901

8

funeral flowers, and these cheese snacks are the funeral food.'

Phillipa looked at Miss Blacklock in a puzzled way.

'Is this a joke?' she asked.

'It's a very nasty joke,' said Dora Bunner with energy.

'Show Phillipa the advertisement,' said Miss Blacklock. 'I must go and shut up the hens. It's dark.' She went out.

'Won't somebody tell me what's happening?' cried Phillipa.

Everybody tried to tell her at once – nobody could find the *Gazette* to show her because Mitzi had taken it into the kitchen.

Miss Blacklock returned a few minutes later.

'There,' she said, 'that's done.' She glanced at the clock. 'Twenty-past six. Somebody ought to be here soon.' She looked at the table with the sherry and cheese snacks laid out on it. 'Patrick, please move that table round the corner, near the window. I don't want it to be obvious that I'm expecting people.'

'Now we can pretend to be quite surprised when somebody arrives,' said Julia.

Miss Blacklock had picked up the sherry bottle. She stood holding it uncertainly in her hand.

'There's half a bottle there,' said Patrick. 'It's enough.'

'Oh, yes – yes …' Miss Blacklock hesitated and her face turned a little red. 'Patrick, would you mind … there's a new bottle in the kitchen. Could you bring it? I – we – could have a new bottle. This – this has been opened for some time.'

Patrick went to the kitchen and returned with the new bottle. He looked curiously at Miss Blacklock as he put it on the table.

'You're taking this seriously, aren't you?' he asked gently. 'You think the sherry in the old bottle might be poisoned?'

'Oh!' said Dora Bunner, shocked. 'Surely you can't imagine –'

'Ssh,' said Miss Blacklock quickly. 'That's the doorbell. You see, I knew people would come.'

♦

Mitzi opened the sitting-room door and showed in Colonel and Mrs Easterbrook.

'I hope you don't mind us calling round,' said Colonel Easterbrook in a voice that was too loud and cheerful. (Julia laughed softly.) 'We were just passing this way. I notice you've got your central heating on. We haven't started ours yet.'

'What beautiful roses!' cried Mrs Easterbrook.

'They're rather old, really,' said Julia.

Mitzi opened the door again and said, 'Here are the ladies from Boulders.'

'Good evening,' said Miss Hinchcliffe, walking over and shaking Miss Blacklock's hand firmly. 'I said to Amy, "Let's just call in at Little Paddocks!" I wanted to ask about your hens.'

'It's getting dark so early now, isn't it?' said Miss Murgatroyd to Patrick. 'What *lovely* roses!'

'They're old!' said Julia.

'You've got your central heating on,' said Miss Hinchcliffe in an accusing way. 'It's very early.'

'The house gets so cold at this time of year,' said Miss Blacklock.

The door opened again and Mrs Swettenham came in. She was followed by Edmund, who looked angry and uncomfortable.

'Here we are!' said Mrs Swettenham, looking around her with open curiosity. 'I just thought I'd come and ask if you wanted a cat, Miss Blacklock. What *lovely* roses!' she added.

'Have you got your central heating on?' asked Edmund.

'Don't people say the same old things?' said Julia quietly.

Once more the door opened, and Mrs Harmon came in. She had put on a hat in an attempt to be fashionable.

'Hello, Miss Blacklock!' she cried, smiling all over her round face. 'I'm not too late, am I? When does the murder begin?'

Everybody made little noises of shock. Julia laughed softly.

'Julian is really cross that he can't be here,' said Mrs Harmon. 'He *loves* murders.'

Miss Blacklock smiled at Mrs Harmon, and looked at the clock over the fireplace.

'If it's going to begin,' she said cheerfully, 'it ought to begin soon. It's almost half past six. But let's have a glass of sherry.'

Patrick went quickly to get the sherry bottle. Miss Blacklock went to the small table by the wall where the cigarette-box was.

'I'd love some sherry,' said Mrs Harmon. 'But what do you mean by *if*?'

'Well,' said Miss Blacklock, 'I know as little about all this as you do. I don't know what –'

She turned her head as the little clock over the fireplace began to strike. It had a sweet bell-like sound. Everybody was silent and nobody moved. They stared at the clock.

As the last note died away, all the lights went out.

Cries of delight were heard in the darkness. 'It's beginning,' cried Mrs Harmon happily.

'Oh, I don't like it!' cried out Dora Bunner.

'How terribly, terribly frightening!' said other voices.

Then, with a crash, the door swung open. A powerful torch shone quickly round the room. A man's voice, which sounded just like the voice of an actor in the cinema, said, 'Put your hands up! Put them up, I tell you!'

Everybody put their hands willingly above their heads.

'Isn't it wonderful?' said a female voice. 'I'm *so* excited!'

And then suddenly there was the noise of a gun. It fired twice.

Suddenly the game was no longer a game. Somebody screamed … The figure in the doorway turned round and seemed to hesitate. A third shot rang out and the figure fell to the ground. The torch dropped and went out. There was darkness once more. And gently, the sitting-room door swung shut.

♦

Inside the sitting-room, everybody was speaking at once.

'Lights.' 'Can't you find the switch?' 'Who's got a lighter?' 'Oh, I don't *like* it, I don't *like* it.' 'But those shots were *real*!' 'It was a *real* gun he had.' 'Was it a burglar?' 'Oh, Archie, I want to get out of here.' 'Please, has somebody got a lighter?'

And then, almost at the same moment, two cigarette lighters were switched on and burned with small, steady flames.

Everybody looked at everyone else with shocked faces. Against the wall by the table, Miss Blacklock stood with her hand to her face. Something dark was running over her fingers.

'Try the light switch, Swettenham,' said Colonel Easterbrook.

Edmund, near the door, obediently moved the switch up and down. But the lights didn't go on.

'Who's making that terrible noise?' asked the Colonel.

A female voice had been screaming steadily from somewhere beyond the closed door. At the same time the sound of someone beating on a door was heard.

Dora Bunner, who had been crying quietly, cried out, 'It's Mitzi. Somebody's murdering Mitzi …'

The Colonel was already opening the sitting-room door. He and Edmund, carrying cigarette lighters, stepped into the hall. They almost fell over a figure lying there.

'She's in the dining-room,' said Edmund.

The dining-room was just across the hall. Someone was beating on the door and screaming.

'She's been locked in,' said Edmund, bending down. He turned the key and Mitzi rushed out like a wild animal, still screaming. The dining-room light was still on, and Mitzi's dark shape stood out against the light, mad with terror.

'Be quiet, Mitzi,' said Miss Blacklock.

'Stop it,' said Edmund. Then he leaned forward and hit her across the face. At once Mitzi was shocked into silence.

'Get some candles,' said Miss Blacklock. 'They're in the kitchen cupboard. Patrick, you know where the fusebox is?

Perhaps a fuse needs mending.'

'Right,' said Patrick. 'I'll see what I can do.'

Miss Blacklock had moved forward into the light thrown from the dining-room. Dora Bunner gave a cry and Mitzi started to scream again.

'The blood, the *blood*!' she cried. 'You are shot – Miss Blacklock, you will bleed to death.'

'Don't be so stupid,' said Miss Blacklock crossly. 'I'm hardly hurt at all. It just hit my ear.'

'But, Aunt Letty,' said Julia, 'the blood.'

Miss Blacklock's white blouse was covered with blood.

'Ears always bleed,' said Miss Blacklock. 'I remember having my hair cut as a child when the hairdresser cut my ear by mistake. There was a whole bowl of blood. But we *must* have some light.'

'I'll get candles,' said Mitzi.

Julia went with her and they came back with several candles.

'Now let's have a look at our criminal,' said the Colonel. 'Hold the candles down low, will you, Swettenham?'

'I'll come to the other side,' said Phillipa. She held the candles with a steady hand, and Colonel Easterbrook knelt down.

The figure lying on the ground was wearing a long black coat and hat. There was a black mask over his face and he wore black cotton gloves. The hat had slipped back, showing fair hair.

Colonel Easterbrook turned him over and felt for his heart … then he looked down at his hands. They were sticky and red.

'He's shot himself,' he said.

'Is he badly hurt?' asked Miss Blacklock.

'Hmm. I'm afraid he's dead. If I could see better …'

At that moment, seemingly by magic, the lights came on again. Everybody felt very strange as they realised that violent death had just happened in their presence. Colonel Easterbrook's hand was red. Blood was running down Miss Blacklock's blouse. The body of the criminal lay at their feet …

Patrick, coming from the dining-room, said, 'Only one fuse had gone ...' He stopped.

Colonel Easterbrook pulled at the mask.

'We'd better see who the man is,' he said. 'Though I don't suppose it's anyone we know ...' He took the mask off.

Everyone moved forward to have a look.

'He's quite young,' said Mrs Harmon with pity in her voice.

Suddenly Dora Bunner cried out excitedly, 'Letty, Letty, it's the young man from the Spa Hotel in Medenham Wells. He came here and wanted you to give him money to get back to Switzerland, and you refused. Oh dear, he almost killed you ...'

Miss Blacklock, in command of the situation, said, 'Patrick, take Bunny into the dining-room and give her a drink. Julia, run up to the bathroom and bring me a bandage to stop the bleeding. Patrick, will you phone the police at once?'

Chapter 3   The Young Man from Switzerland

The Chief Constable of Middleshire, George Rydesdale, was a quiet man who was more used to listening than talking. He was listening now to Detective-Inspector Dermot Craddock. Craddock was officially in charge of the case.

'Do you know who the dead man is?' asked Rydesdale.

'Yes, sir,' replied Craddock. 'Rudi Scherz. Swiss. Employed at the Royal Spa Hotel, Medenham Wells, as a receptionist.'

The door opened, and the Chief Constable looked up.

'Come in, Henry,' he said. 'We've got something here that's a little unusual.'

A tall, grey-haired man came in. He was Sir Henry Clithering, the retired head of Scotland Yard⋆.

⋆ Scotland Yard: the main building for London's police officers

Craddock took out the *Chipping Cleghorn Gazette*, and showed Sir Henry the advertisement about the murder.

'Do we know who put this advertisement in the newspaper?' asked Rydesdale.

'From the description of the man who handed it in, sir, it was Rudi Scherz himself – on Wednesday.'

'What sort of a place is Chipping Cleghorn?' asked Sir Henry.

'A large and attractive village. The cottages there were owned by farm workers in the past. But now they're lived in by retired couples and older ladies.'

'It's a pity that *my* old lady isn't here,' said Sir Henry. 'She would love to help in a situation like this!'

'Who is your old lady, Henry? An aunt?'

'No,' Sir Henry sighed. 'She's just the finest detective God ever made.'

'I'll remember that,' said Detective-Inspector Craddock.

'Was there anything worth stealing in the house?' asked Sir Henry. 'Did Miss Blacklock keep much money there?'

'She says not, sir. About five pounds, I understand.'

'So the man wasn't interested in money,' said Sir Henry. 'He wanted the fun of acting out a robbery, perhaps. Like in films. How did he manage to shoot himself?'

'According to the first medical report, the gun was fired very close to him,' said Craddock. 'But we don't know whether it was an accident or whether he killed himself deliberately.'

'You'll have to question the witnesses very carefully,' said Sir Henry, 'and make them say exactly what they saw.'

'They probably all saw something different,' said Detective-Inspector Craddock sadly.

'It's very interesting what people see,' said Sir Henry. 'But it's even more interesting what they *don't* see. Craddock, go to the Royal Spa Hotel. See what you can find out about Rudi Scherz.'

♦

At the Royal Spa Hotel, Inspector Craddock was taken straight to the manager's office. The manager greeted him warmly.

'This is really a most surprising business,' he said. 'Scherz seemed a very ordinary, pleasant young man.'

'How long has he been with you?' asked Craddock.

'A little over three months.'

'And were you satisfied with him?'

The manager hesitated. Then he said, rather unwillingly, 'Well, once or twice there was trouble about the bills. He charged guests for things that they hadn't used.'

'So when the guests paid too much on their bills, he put the extra money in his own pocket?' asked Craddock.

'Something like that ... but perhaps he just made careless mistakes. And missing money was always paid back.'

'Any women in his life?'

'One of the restaurant waitresses. Her name's Myrna Harris.'

'I'd better have a talk with her.'

Myrna Harris was a pretty girl with red hair. She was nervous and uncomfortable about being interviewed by the police.

'I don't know anything about it, sir. Nothing,' she said. 'If I'd known what Rudi was like, I'd never have gone out with him.'

'Did you know him well?' asked Craddock.

'Oh, we were friendly – that's all, just friendly. Sometimes Rudi liked to talk big, but I didn't believe all the things he said.'

'Talk big, Miss Harris? What do you mean?'

'Well, about how rich his family were in Switzerland – and how important. But he never seemed to have much money.'

'Did you go out with him a lot?'

'Yes – well – yes, I did. He was very polite and he knew how to look after a girl. The best seats at the cinema. And he sometimes bought me flowers. And he was a lovely dancer.'

'Did he mention this Miss Blacklock to you at all?'

'She comes and has lunch here sometimes, doesn't she? And she stayed here once. But I don't think Rudi ever mentioned her.'

'Did he mention Chipping Cleghorn?'

Craddock thought that a nervous look came into Myrna Harris's eyes, but he couldn't be sure.

'I don't think so … He asked once about what time buses went – but I can't remember if that was buses to Chipping Cleghorn.'

She couldn't tell Craddock anything more.

♦

Little Paddocks was very much as Detective-Inspector Craddock had imagined. There were hens and some attractive flowers in the garden. As Craddock's car stopped at the front door, Sergeant Fletcher came round the side of the house.

'We've finished checking the house, sir. Scherz didn't leave any fingerprints. He wore gloves, of course. No signs of any of the doors or windows being forced open. He came from Medenham on the bus, arriving here at six o'clock. He probably walked in through the front door. Miss Blacklock states that the door isn't usually locked until the house is shut for the night. The cook says that the front door was locked all afternoon – but she's a very difficult person. From somewhere in Central Europe.'

Craddock noticed two enormous, frightened black eyes looking out of a window by the front door.

'That's her there?'

'That's right, sir.'

The face disappeared. Craddock rang the front-door bell. After a long wait, the door was opened by a good-looking young woman with dark-brown hair and a bored expression.

'Detective-Inspector Craddock,' said Craddock.

The girl stared at him coolly out of very attractive blue eyes.

'Come in. Miss Blacklock is expecting you.'

She led the way down a hall which was long and narrow and full of doors. Then she threw open a door on the left.

'Inspector Craddock, Aunt Letty.' She left, shutting the door.

Craddock saw a tall active-looking woman of about sixty with grey hair, sharp grey eyes and a strong, intelligent face. There was a bandage on her left ear. Close beside her was a woman of about the same age. She had an eager, round face and untidy hair. Craddock already knew who she was. He had read the notes that Sergeant Fletcher had made in his notebook. Beside Dora's name, he had written 'slightly mad'.

'Good morning, Inspector Craddock,' said Miss Blacklock. Her voice was pleasant and well-educated. 'This is my friend, Miss Bunner, who helps me run the house.'

Craddock glanced quickly around the room. There were two long windows in this room, a large window in the other … chairs … sofa … centre table with a big bowl of roses. The only unusual thing was a small silver vase with dead violets in it on a small table near the wall. He could not imagine that Miss Blacklock would normally have dead flowers in a room.

'Is this the room in which the shooting happened?'

'Yes.'

'When did you first see the dead man – Rudi Scherz?'

'Is that his name?' Miss Blacklock looked slightly surprised. 'I first met him in Medenham Spa about three weeks ago. We – Miss Bunner and I – were having lunch at the Royal Spa Hotel. As we were leaving, I heard my name spoken. It was this young man. He said, "It is Miss Blacklock, is it not?" He then said that he was the son of the owner of the Hotel des Alpes in Montreux. My sister and I stayed there during the war.'

'And did you remember him, Miss Blacklock?'

'No. These boys at hotel reception desks all look the same.'

'And your next meeting?' asked Craddock.

'About – yes, it was ten days ago, he suddenly came to the

house. I was very surprised to see him. He told me that his mother was ill and he needed money to return to Switzerland.'

'But Letty didn't give it to him,' said Miss Bunner.

'I didn't believe his story,' said Miss Blacklock with energy. 'Why didn't he get the money from his father?' She paused and said, 'I'm not a hard-hearted person, but I was secretary for many years to a big businessman. One learns to suspect stories from people asking for money.'

'Do you think now, looking back on it, that he came here just as an excuse to look at the house?' asked Craddock.

'That's exactly what I do think – now,' said Miss Blacklock. 'When he left, he opened the front door for me, but I think he just wanted to have a look at the lock.'

'And there is also a side door to the garden, I understand?'

'Yes. I went through it to shut up the hens just before people arrived. I locked it when I came in – at a quarter-past six.'

'So Scherz probably walked in quite easily through the front door. Or perhaps he came in while you were shutting up the hens. Yes, that all seems quite clear.'

'I'm sorry, it's not clear at all,' said Miss Blacklock. 'Why would anyone come here and act out a silly kind of robbery?'

'Do you keep much money or jewellery in the house?'

'About five pounds in that desk there, and perhaps a pound or two in my purse. And very little jewellery.'

'It wasn't burglary at all!' cried Miss Bunner. 'I've told you that, Letty. It was *revenge* because you wouldn't give him that money! He shot at you deliberately – twice.'

'What happened last night, Miss Blacklock?' asked Craddock.

'The clock struck,' said Miss Blacklock. 'We all listened to it without saying anything. Then, suddenly, the lights went out.'

'Was there a flash first, or a noise?'

'I don't think so.'

'I'm sure there was a flash,' said Dora Bunner. '*And* a cracking noise. Dangerous!'

'And then the door opened – '

'Which door? There are two in the room.'

'Oh, this door in here. The one in the other room doesn't open. It's a false door. There he was – a masked man with a gun. I thought it was a silly joke. He said something – I forget what – '

'Hands up or I shoot!' cried Miss Bunner.

'Something like that,' said Miss Blacklock doubtfully. 'And then he shone a torch right in my eyes. I couldn't see anything because of the bright light. And then I heard a bullet go past me and hit the wall by my head. Somebody screamed. I felt a burning pain in my ear, and heard the second shot.'

'And what happened next, Miss Blacklock?'

'It's difficult to say – I was so shocked by the pain and the surprise. The figure turned away and seemed to hesitate, and then there was another shot and everybody began calling out.'

'Where were you standing, Miss Blacklock?'

'She was over by the table. She had that vase of violets in her hand,' said Miss Bunner breathlessly.

'I was over here.' Miss Blacklock went over to the table by the wall. 'Actually it was the cigarette-box that I had in my hand.'

Inspector Craddock examined the wall. The two bullet holes showed plainly. The police had already taken the bullets out.

'He *did* shoot at her,' said Miss Bunner. 'I saw him. He shone the torch on everybody until he found her. He *meant* to kill you, Letty. Then he shot himself.'

'Miss Blacklock, until the gun was fired, you thought the whole business was a joke? Who do you think was responsible?'

'You thought Patrick had done it at first,' Dora Bunner said.

'Patrick?' asked the Inspector sharply.

'My young cousin, Patrick Simmons,' Miss Blacklock continued, annoyed with her friend. 'I did think when I saw the advertisement that it might be Patrick playing a joke.'

'And then you were worried, Letty,' said Miss Bunner. 'And you were quite right. A murder was announced – *your* murder!'

Dora Bunner was shaking as she spoke. Miss Blacklock put her hand on Dora's shoulder.

'It's all right, Dora dear – don't get excited. Everything's all right.' She added, 'You know I depend on you, Dora, to help me look after the house. Isn't it the day for the laundry to come?'

'Oh yes, Letty, it is. I'll go and check at once.'

'And take those violets away,' said Miss Blacklock. 'There's nothing I hate more than dead flowers.'

'Oh dear, I probably forgot to put any water in the vase,' said Dora Bunner. 'I'm always forgetting things.'

She hurried out, looking happy again.

'She's not very strong,' said Miss Blacklock, 'and excitement is bad for her. Is there anything else you want to know?'

'I want to know how many people live in your house.'

'Yes, well, in addition to myself and Dora Bunner, I have two young cousins living here at present – Patrick and Julia Simmons. They call me Aunt Letty, but actually their mother was my second cousin. They've only been here for the last two months. Their mother wrote and asked me if they could possibly come as paying guests – Julia is training at Milchester Hospital, and Patrick is studying for an engineering degree at Milchester University. I was very glad to have them here.'

'Then there is a Mrs Haymes, I believe?'

'Yes. She works as an assistant gardener at Dayas Hall, Mrs Lucas's place. She's a very nice girl. Her husband was killed in Italy, and she has a boy of eight who is away at school, but who comes here in the holidays.'

'And what about people who work for you?'

'I have a cook, Mitzi, who had to escape from Europe. You'll find her rather difficult. She thinks people are trying to kill her.'

Craddock nodded. Beside Mitzi's name, Sergeant Fletcher

had written one word in his notebook – 'liar'.

'Mitzi does make up stories,' said Miss Blacklock 'She had a bad shock and did see one of her relations killed. And now she just invents and exaggerates things to make us sympathetic.' She smiled. 'But when she wants to, she can cook very nicely.'

'I'll try not to upset her,' said Craddock. 'Was that Miss Julia Simmons who opened the door to me?'

'Yes. Would you like to see her? Patrick has gone out.'

'Thank you. I'd like to see Miss Simmons now if I may.'

Chapter 4   Questions and Answers

Julia came into the room and sat down in the chair. Miss Blacklock had already left the room. Julia seemed very calm.

'Please tell me about last night, Miss Simmons,' said Craddock.

'Well, a lot of annoying people came … There was Colonel and Mrs Easterbrook, Miss Hinchcliffe and Miss Murgatroyd, Mrs Swettenham and Edmund Swettenham, and Mrs Harmon, Reverend Harmon's wife. And if you want to know what they said – they all said the same thing in turn. "I see you've got your central heating on" and "What *lovely* roses!"'

Craddock tried not to smile. Julia's imitation was very good.

'Only Mrs Harmon asked openly when the murder was going to happen. And then the clock struck and just as it finished, the lights went out, the door was thrown open and a masked figure said, "Put your hands up!" or something like that. It was exactly like a bad film. Really quite silly. And then he fired two shots at Aunt Letty, and suddenly it wasn't silly any more.'

'Where was everybody when the lights went out?'

'Oh, just standing and talking. Most people were in this room, although Patrick had gone into the far room to get the sherry. I think I was by the window. Aunt Letty went to get the cigarettes. They were on that small table by the wall.'

'The man had a powerful torch. What did he do with it?'

'Well, he shone it on us. It was horribly bright.'

'Did he hold the torch steady, or did he move it around?'

Julia thought. 'He moved it,' she said slowly. 'It was full in my eyes and then it went around the room and then the shots came. Two shots. Mitzi began screaming from somewhere. Then his torch went out and there was another shot. And then the door closed and we were all in the dark, not knowing what to do.'

'Do you think he was aiming at Miss Blacklock?'

Julia seemed a little surprised.

'You mean, trying to attack Aunt Letty? Oh, I shouldn't think so … I mean, if he'd wanted to shoot her, there were lots of more suitable opportunities. Why didn't he shoot her when she was out walking alone in the country?'

'Thank you, Miss Simmons,' said Craddock with a sigh. 'I'd better go and see Mitzi now.'

Craddock and Sergeant Fletcher found Mitzi in the kitchen, cooking. She looked up, unsmiling, as they entered. Her black hair hung over her eyes.

'What do you come in my kitchen for, Mr Policeman? You are police, yes? You come to make me say things, but I shall say *nothing*. You will pull off my fingernails and put lighted matches on my skin. But I will not speak, do you hear?'

Craddock looked at her. Finally he sighed and said, 'OK, get your hat and coat. I haven't got my nail-pulling equipment with me. We keep all that down at the police station.'

'But I do not want to come,' screamed Mitzi, moving away.

'Then you'll answer my questions politely. I want you to tell me what happened last night.'

'I was nervous. Very nervous. All that evening, I hear things. People moving around. I take the sherry and the glasses into the sitting-room. Then the bell rings and I answer the door. Again and again I answer the door. And then I go back into the kitchen, and I start to polish the silver. And then, suddenly – I hear shots. I run through the dining-room, and then there comes another shot and a big noise, out there in the hall, and I turn the door handle, but it is locked outside. I am shut in there like a rat. And I am mad with fear. I scream and scream and I beat on the door. And at last – at last – they turn the key and let me out. And then I bring candles, and the lights go on, and I see blood – blood! Ach, the blood! It is not the first time I have seen blood –'

'Yes,' said Inspector Craddock. 'Thank you very much.'

'And now you can take me to prison!' said Mitzi.

'Not today,' said Inspector Craddock.

As Craddock and Fletcher went through the hall to the front door, it was thrown open. A tall, handsome young man came in.

'Mr Patrick Simmons?'

'Quite right, Inspector. You're the Inspector, aren't you?'

'Yes, Mr Simmons. Can I have a word with you, please?'

'I am innocent, Inspector. I swear I am innocent.'

'Now, Mr Simmons, don't joke with me. Will you describe what happened last night?'

'Well, Aunt Letty opened a new bottle of sherry –'

Craddock interrupted.

'A new bottle? Was there an old one?'

'Yes, half full. But Aunt Letty didn't seem to want it.'

'Was she nervous, then?'

'Oh, not really. She's extremely sensible. It was Bunny, I think, who had made her nervous. She had been frightened all day.'

'It seems that Miss Blacklock thought, when she first read that advertisement, that you had put it there. Why?'

'Oh, I always get blamed for everything around here.'

'Have you ever seen or spoken to Rudi Scherz?'

'I've never seen him in my life.'

'Tell me what happened.'

24

'I'd just gone to fetch the drinks when the lights went out. I turned round and there was a man in the doorway saying, "Put up your hands." He starts firing a gun, and then he goes down with a crash and his torch goes out, and we're in the dark again.'

'Do you think the attacker was aiming at Miss Blacklock?'

'Ah, how could I tell? I think he just fired his gun as a joke.'

'And then he shot himself?'

'It could be.'

'Thank you, Mr Simmons. I want to interview the other people who were here last night. Which would be the best order?'

'Well, our Phillipa – Mrs Haymes – works at Dayas Hall. The gates to it are nearly opposite our gate.'

♦

Phillipa Haymes was picking apples in the gardens of Dayas Hall. She stood looking at Craddock in surprise.

'Good morning, Mrs Haymes. I'm Inspector Craddock of the Middleshire Police. I wanted to have a word with you. What time did you come home from work last night?'

'At about half past five.'

'You came in by which door?'

'The side door. I always come in that way.'

'The door was unlocked?'

'Yes. I locked it when I came in.'

'Do you always do that?'

'I've been doing it for the last week. You see, it gets dark at six. Miss Blacklock goes out to shut up the hens sometime in the evening, but she very often goes out through the kitchen door.'

'And what did you do when you came in?'

'I took off my muddy shoes, and went upstairs and had a bath. Then I came down and found that a party was taking place. I hadn't known anything about the advertisement until then.'

'Please describe what happened during the hold–up.'

'Well, the lights went out suddenly – I was standing by the fireplace. Then the door was thrown open and a man shone a torch on us and waved a gun around and told us to put our hands up. And then the gun went off. The shots were very loud and I was really frightened. And then Mitzi started screaming.'

'Did the man move the torch?'

'Oh, yes, all round the room.'

'And after that, Mrs Haymes?'

'Oh, there was terrible confusion. Edmund Swettenham and Patrick Simmons went out into the hall and we followed, and someone opened the dining-room door – and Edmund hit Mitzi to stop her screaming, and after that it wasn't so bad.'

'You saw the body of the dead man? Was he known to you?'

'No. I'd never seen him before.'

'Do you think he shot himself deliberately?'

'I have absolutely no idea.'

'Thank you, Mrs Haymes. One more thing. Do you have any valuable jewellery? Is there anything of value in the house?'

Phillipa shook her head.

'My wedding ring. And there's some quite nice silver, but nothing unusual.'

'Thank you, Mrs Haymes.'

♦

'It was terrible,' said Mrs Swettenham happily. 'Quite terrible.'

'Do you remember what you were doing when the lights went out, Mrs Swettenham?' asked the Inspector.

'Well, we were all standing around and wondering what was going to happen. And then the door opened – just a dark figure standing there with a gun and that blinding light and a voice saying, "Your money or your life!" And then a minute later, it was *all terrible*. Real bullets, just whistling past our ears!'

'Where were you sitting or standing at the time?'

'I was somewhere over by the window or near the fireplace, because I know I was quite near the clock when it struck. Such an exciting moment! Waiting to see if anything might happen.'

'Was the torch turned full on you?' asked Craddock.

'It was right in my eyes. I couldn't see anything.'

'Did the man hold it still, or did he move it around?'

'Oh, I don't really know. Which did he do, Edmund?'

'He moved it rather slowly over us all, to see what we were all doing, I suppose,' replied Edmund.

'And where exactly in the room were you, Mr Swettenham?'

'I'd been talking to Julia Simmons. We were both standing up in the middle of the room – the long room.'

'Do you think the third shot was an accident?'

'I've no idea. The man seemed to turn round very quickly and then fall – but it was all very confused. We couldn't see anything. And then that foreign girl started screaming.'

'I understand it was you who unlocked the dining-room door and let her out? Was the door definitely locked on the outside?'

Edmund looked at him curiously.

'Certainly it was. Why, you don't imagine –?'

'I just want to be sure of what happened. Thank you.'

♦

Inspector Craddock was forced to spend quite a long time with Colonel and Mrs Easterbrook. He had to listen to the Colonel's long description of the psychology of the criminal's mind.

'I've got very wide experience of criminal psychology,' said the Colonel. 'This man wanted to carry out a robbery with violence in front of an audience, just like in the cinema. And then he becomes a killer. He shoots – blindly –'

Inspector Craddock caught gladly at a word.

'You say "blindly". You didn't think he was firing at one particular thing – at Miss Blacklock, for example?'

27

'No, no. He was just firing blindly. The bullet hits someone and he becomes frightened. So then he turns the gun on himself.'

'It really is wonderful,' said Mrs Easterbrook in a voice warm with admiration, 'how you know what happened, Archie.'

Inspector Craddock thought it was wonderful too, but he was not quite as full of admiration for Colonel Easterbrook.

'Exactly where were you in the room, Colonel Easterbrook, when the actual shooting took place?' he asked.

'My wife and I were near a centre table with flowers on it.'

'I caught hold of your arm, didn't I, Archie, when it happened? I was so frightened. I just had to hold on to you.'

'Poor little bird,' said the Colonel playfully.

♦

Inspector Craddock went to see Miss Hinchcliffe and Miss Murgatroyd. Miss Hinchcliffe was feeding the pigs.

'Where were you exactly when the shooting started?' he asked.

'I was leaning up against the fireplace, hoping that someone would offer me a drink soon,' replied Miss Hinchcliffe at once.

'Do you think that the shots were fired blindly, or aimed carefully at one particular person?'

'You mean aimed at Letty Blacklock? How should I know? I only know that the lights went out, and then that torch went round. I thought to myself, "If that young fool Patrick Simmons is playing jokes with real bullets, somebody will get hurt."'

'You thought it was Patrick Simmons?'

'Well, it seemed likely. Patrick's a wild boy.'

Miss Murgatroyd came in. She had walked quickly from the garden, and her clothes and hair were untidy. Her round, good-natured face was smiling. Craddock introduced himself.

'Where were you at the time of the crime, that's what he wants to know, Amy,' said Miss Hinchcliffe, smiling.

'I'd been admiring the roses,' said Miss Murgatroyd. 'And

then it all happened. Everything was so confused in the dark, and that terrible screaming. I thought *she* was being murdered – I mean the foreign girl. I didn't even know there was a man. It was just a voice, you know, saying "Put them up, please."'

'I suggest you go and interview Mrs Harmon next,' said Miss Hinchcliffe. 'The vicarage is near here.'

As they watched the Inspector and Sergeant Fletcher walk away, Amy Murgatroyd said breathlessly:

'Oh, was I very awful? I do get so confused.'

'Not at all,' Miss Hinchcliffe smiled. 'You did very well.'

♦

Inspector Craddock looked around Mrs Harmon's large sitting-room with a sense of pleasure. It reminded him a little of his own home. He also thought that Mrs Harmon was a pleasant woman.

But she said at once, 'I shan't be any help to you because I shut my eyes. I hate looking into a bright light. And when I heard the shots, I closed my eyes even more tightly. I don't like bangs.'

'What else did you hear?' asked the Inspector.

'Doors opening and shutting and Mitzi and Bunny screaming. When the bangs had stopped, I opened my eyes. Everyone was out in the hall then, with candles. And then the lights came on. And there was the man, lying there dead, with a gun beside him. It didn't seem to make *sense*, somehow.'

It did not make sense to the Inspector, either.

Chapter 5   Miss Marple Arrives

Rydesdale, the Chief Constable, had contacted the police in Switzerland about Rudi Scherz. He showed their answer to Inspector Craddock.

'He had a police record,' Rydesdale said. 'He stole jewellery and other things. He was definitely dishonest in a small way. But small things lead to large things.'

'I'm worried, sir,' said Craddock. 'It just doesn't make sense.'

'Do you think that somebody is lying to you?'

'I think the foreign girl knows more than she's telling us. And Miss Bunner thinks that Scherz was trying to kill Miss Blacklock.'

'Don't worry, Craddock,' said the Chief Constable. 'I'm taking you to lunch at the Royal Spa Hotel with Sir Henry and myself.' He stopped as Sir Henry entered the room. 'Ah, Sir Henry. We've received a letter from a woman staying at the Royal Spa Hotel. She says there's something we might like to know in connection with this Chipping Cleghorn business. Her name is Jane – Murple – no, Marple, Jane Marple.'

'But I know Miss Marple,' said Sir Henry. 'She's the old lady I mentioned before – the one who is so good at solving crimes.'

'Well,' said Rydesdale, 'I'll be glad to meet her. Let's go! We'll lunch at the Royal Spa and we'll interview Miss Marple.'

♦

Miss Jane Marple was older than Craddock had imagined. She had snow-white hair, a pink face and very soft, innocent eyes. She was delighted to see Sir Henry, and very pleased to meet Chief Constable Rydesdale and Detective-Inspector Craddock.

'But really, Sir Henry, how fortunate … how very fortunate. So long since I've seen you.'

'Now, Miss Marple, let's hear what you have to tell us,' said the Chief Constable.

'It was a cheque,' she said at once. 'The young man at the desk changed it. The young man who, they say, is responsible for that hold-up and shot himself. I have it here.' Miss Marple took a cheque out of her bag and laid it on the table. 'It came this morning with my other cheques from the bank. You can see, it was for seven pounds and he changed it to seventeen. It's very cleverly done. I think he'd often done it before, don't you?'

'And perhaps he reminded you of someone?' asked Sir Henry with a smile. He knew that Miss Marple often compared the behaviour of criminals with the ways of people in her village.

'Yes, he *did*. Fred Tyler, at the fish shop. Fred always put an extra "1" before the figures in the money column on the bills. Lots of people never added up their bill, and so they never noticed. Then he put the extra money in his pocket.

Well, the first week I was staying here at the Royal Spa, there was a mistake in my bill. I showed the young man, and he apologised very nicely. But after that I didn't trust him. He didn't look honest.'

'He had a police record in Switzerland,' said Rydesdale.

'He was very friendly with the little red-haired waitress from the dining-room,' said Miss Marple. 'Has she told you all she knows?' she asked suddenly, turning to Craddock.

'I'm not absolutely sure,' said Craddock carefully.

'She's looking very worried,' said Miss Marple. 'She brought me the wrong food at breakfast, and forgot the milk jug. But I expect' – her blue eyes looked into the handsome face of Detective-Inspector Craddock – 'that you will be able to persuade her to tell you all she knows. Perhaps he told her who it was. I mean, who instructed him to do the hold-up.'

Rydesdale stared at her.

'So you think someone instructed him?'

Miss Marple's eyes widened in surprise.

'Oh, but surely – I mean … Here's an attractive young man who steals a little bit here and there. And then suddenly he goes off, with a gun, and holds up a room full of people, and shoots at someone. That wasn't like him at all! He wasn't that kind of person. It doesn't make *sense*.'

Craddock breathed in sharply. That was what Mrs Harmon had said. What he himself felt. *It didn't make sense.*

'What did happen, then, Miss Marple?' he asked.

'But how should I know what happened?' said Miss Marple in surprise. 'I have no accurate information.'

'Can we allow Miss Marple to read the notes about the case?' Sir Henry asked Rydesdale.

'Yes,' replied Rydesdale. He handed her some typewritten sheets of paper. 'Read these. It won't take you long.'

Miss Marple read the notes in silence.

'It's very interesting,' she said. 'All the different things that people say. The things they see – or think that they see.'

Craddock felt disappointed. Was that all that Sir Henry's famous Miss Marple could say? He felt annoyed with her.

'All these people saw the same thing,' said Craddock. 'They saw a masked man with a gun and a torch. They *saw* him.'

'But surely,' said Miss Marple gently, 'they didn't – actually – see anything at all … ' Her face shone pink, and her eyes were as bright and pleased as a child's. 'There wasn't any light on in the hall, was there? So if a man stood in the doorway and flashed a powerful torch into the room, *nobody could see anything except the torch*, could they?'

Rydesdale stared at her in surprise. Her face became pinker.

'I'm not very clever about American phrases,' she said, 'but I think that Rudi Scherz was what they call a "fall guy". A "fall guy" is someone who will be blamed for someone else's crime. Rudi Scherz seems to me exactly the right type for that. Rather stupid, and willing to believe anything.

'I think he was told it was a joke. He was paid for doing it, of course. Paid to put an advertisement in the newspaper, to go to the house and look at it, and then to go there in a mask and a black coat, waving a torch and crying "Hands up!"'

'And to fire a gun?' asked Rydesdale.

'No, no,' said Miss Marple. 'He never had a gun. I think that after he'd called "Hands up", somebody came up quietly behind him in the darkness and fired those two shots over his shoulder. It frightened him and he turned around. The other person shot him and then let the gun drop beside him.'

'It's a possible theory,' Sir Henry said softly.

'But who is this mysterious Mr X?' said Rydesdale.

'You'll have to find out from Miss Blacklock who wanted to kill her. But first, talk to that girl Myrna Harris. It's possible that Rudi Scherz told her who suggested the plan to him.'

'I'll see her now,' said Craddock, getting up. 'Well, Miss Marple, you've certainly given us something to think about.'

'I'm sorry I didn't tell you everything before,' said Myrna Harris to Inspector Craddock. 'I didn't want to get myself in trouble. But I'll tell you *all* about it now, Inspector. Rudi and I were going to the cinema that evening and then he said he wouldn't be able to come. He said not to tell anyone, but there was going to be a party somewhere, and he had to act out a hold-up. Then he showed me the advertisement, and I had to laugh. When I read all about it in the paper, that Rudi had shot someone and then shot himself, I didn't know *what* to do. I didn't even know he had a gun.'

'Who did he say arranged this party?'

'He never said. I thought it was his own idea.'

Later, Rydesdale and Craddock were driving back to Medenham.

'If Miss Marple's theory is correct, there has to be a motive,' said Craddock. 'If it wasn't an ordinary hold-up, it was a cold attempt at murder. But why did somebody try to murder Miss Blacklock? And if they did, the person might try again.'

'That would certainly prove the truth of the theory,' said the Chief Constable. 'Look after Miss Marple, won't you? She's coming to stay at the vicarage at Chipping Cleghorn. It seems that Mrs Harmon is the daughter of an old friend of hers.'

'I'm sorry she's coming,' said Craddock.

'Why? Is she going to get in your way?'

'It's not that, sir, but she's a nice old thing. I wouldn't like anything bad to happen to her …'

♦

Detective-Inspector Craddock went to see Miss Blacklock again.

'I'm sorry to trouble you again, Miss Blacklock, but I have something to tell you. Rudi Scherz was not the son of the owner of the Hotel des Alpes in Montreux. First, he worked in a hospital and then later in a hotel and a shop. He stole small amounts of money and jewellery everywhere.'

'Then I was right when I thought I hadn't seen him before?' asked Miss Blacklock.

'Yes … probably you were pointed out to him at the Royal Spa Hotel and he pretended to recognise you.'

'But why did he want to come to Chipping Cleghorn?' said Miss Blacklock. 'There's nothing of special value in the house.'

'Then it seems, doesn't it, that your friend Miss Bunner was right? He came here to attack you.'

'I knew that advertisement wasn't a joke, Letty,' said Dora Bunner. 'I said so. And look at Mitzi – she was frightened too!'

'I'd like to know more about that young lady,' said Craddock.

'But why would anyone want to murder *me*?' said Miss Blacklock. 'I've got no enemies. I don't know any guilty secrets about anyone. And if you think that Mitzi had something to do with it, that's silly too. She was really frightened when she saw the advertisement in the *Gazette*. Mitzi may be a liar, but she's not a cold-hearted murderer. Go and talk to her. Mrs Harmon is bringing an old lady who is staying with her to tea this afternoon, and I wanted Mitzi to make some little cakes. But I suppose you'll upset her completely. Can't you *possibly* go and suspect somebody else?'

Craddock went out to the kitchen. He asked Mitzi questions

that he had asked her before and received the same answers.

Yes, she had locked the front door soon after four o'clock. No, she hadn't locked the side door.

'Mrs Haymes says she locked the side door when she came in.'

'Ah, and you believe her – oh yes, you believe her.'

'You think Mrs Haymes didn't lock that door?'

'I think she was very careful not to lock it. That young man, he does not work alone. No, he knows where to come, he knows that when he comes, a door will be left open for him – oh, very conveniently open!'

'What are you trying to say?' asked Craddock.

'What is the use of what I say? You will not listen. You say I am a poor foreign girl who tells lies. If I say that I heard him talking with Mrs Haymes – yes, out there in the summerhouse – you will say that I make it up!'

'You couldn't hear what was said in the summerhouse.'

'You are wrong,' screamed Mitzi. 'I go out to the garden to get vegetables. And I hear them talking in there. He says to her, "But where can I hide?" And she says, "I will show you" – and then she says, "At a quarter past six."'

'Why didn't you tell me this the other day?' asked Craddock.

'Because I did not remember – I did not think . . . Only afterwards, I say to myself, it is planned then, planned with her. She is a thief, that Mrs Haymes. Oh, she is bad, that one! Now, how can I cook lunch if you are here, talking, talking, talking? Please leave my kitchen.'

Craddock went obediently, feeling confused. Mitzi told lies, but her story about Phillipa Haymes seemed to contain some truth. He decided to speak to Phillipa.

He crossed the hall and tried to open a door into the sitting-room, but it wouldn't open. Miss Bunner came down the stairs.

'Not that door,' she said. 'It doesn't open. Try the next door to the left. It's very confusing, isn't it? I've often tried the wrong

35

door by mistake. We used to have the hall table against it, but then we moved it along against the wall there.'

'Moved?' asked Craddock. 'How long ago?'

'Well – ten days or a fortnight ago.'

'Is the door a false door?' asked Craddock.

'Oh no, it's a *real* door. It's the door of the small sitting-room, but when the two rooms were made into one room, two doors weren't needed. So this one was locked.'

Craddock tried it again. 'Do you know where the key is?'

'There are a lot of keys in the hall drawer. It's probably there.'

Craddock followed her and found a number of keys pushed back in the drawer. He took one out and went back to the door. The key fitted and turned easily. The door slid open noiselessly.

'This door's been opened quite recently, Miss Bunner. The lock has been oiled.'

'But who would do that?' asked Dora Bunner, shocked.

'That's what I intend to find out,' said Craddock. He thought to himself, 'X – from outside? No – X was here – in this house. X was in the sitting-room that night …'

Chapter 6   Pip and Emma

Miss Blacklock listened to Craddock this time with more attention. She understood what he was telling her about the door.

'You see what this means,' said the Inspector. 'When the lights went out, *anybody in the room the other night* could hurry out of that door, come behind Rudi Scherz and fire at you.'

'Without being seen or heard or noticed?'

'Yes. Remember that when the lights went out, people moved around and were very confused. And they could see nothing except the blinding light of the torch.'

Miss Blacklock said slowly, 'And you think one of those

people – one of my nice, ordinary neighbours – left the room and tried to murder me? *Me*? But *why*?'

'I've a feeling that you must know the answer to that question, Miss Blacklock. Who inherits your money after your death?'

Miss Blacklock said rather unwillingly, 'Patrick and Julia. But I don't believe Patrick and Julia would plan to murder me. And at the moment I don't have very much to leave them. *One* day I might be worth murdering, but not now.'

'What do you mean, Miss Blacklock?' said Craddock.

'Well, one day I may be a very rich woman. You may not know it, but for more than twenty years I was secretary to Randall Goedler.'

Craddock was interested. Randall Goedler had been a big name in the world of business. He had died, if Craddock remembered correctly, in 1937 or 1938.

'He was very rich, wasn't he?' asked Craddock.

'Yes, and he had no children. He left his money to his wife during her lifetime, and after her death, to me. You see, when Randall was starting out on his career, he needed money for a business deal. I had a little money of my own, and I lent it to him. The deal was successful and he became very rich. After that, he treated me like a partner.' Miss Blacklock sighed. 'Then my father died. I had to give up work and go and look after my sister, who was an invalid. Randall died a couple of years later. He left all his money to his wife, Belle. But in his will he stated that if Belle dies before me, I inherit everything. Belle is really a very sweet person, and she was delighted about it. She lives up in Scotland. I haven't seen her for years. You see, I went with my sister to a special hospital in Switzerland just before the war. She died out there. I only came back to England just over a year ago.'

'You said you might be a rich woman very soon. How soon?'

'I heard from the nurse who looks after Belle that Belle is very ill. She may die in a few weeks' time. So you see, Inspector, if Patrick and Julia had wanted to kill me to get my money, they'd be crazy not to wait for a few more weeks.'

'Yes, Miss Blacklock, but what happens if you die before Mrs Goedler? Who inherits the money then?'

'I've never really thought. Pip and Emma, I suppose …'

Craddock stared, and Miss Blacklock smiled.

'They're the children of Randall Goedler's only sister, Sonia. Randall had quarrelled with his sister. She married a man who Randall thought was a criminal. His name was Dmitri Stamfordis. Sonia wrote to Belle after her marriage, telling her that she was extremely happy, and had just had twins. She called them Pip and Emma. The lawyers told Randall that he had to name someone else in his will because I might die before Belle. So he put down Sonia's children's names, only because he couldn't think of anyone else.'

The Inspector looked very serious.

'So if you had been killed the other night,' he said, 'there are two people in the world – Pip and Emma – who would become very rich. These two have a very strong motive for killing you. How old would this brother and sister be?'

'Let me think … I suppose about twenty-five or twenty-six.'

'I think somebody shot at you with the intention of killing you. I think it's possible that the same person may try again. I would like you to be very *very* careful, Miss Blacklock.'

♦

Inspector Craddock went to see Phillipa Haymes again in the garden at Dayas Hall. He looked at her closely. She was a good-looking girl, with pale blonde hair and a rather long face. Her eyes were very blue and steady, and told you nothing at all. The sort of girl, he thought, who would keep a secret well.

'I'm sorry to trouble you again at work, Mrs Haymes,' he said. 'But a certain statement has been made to me about you.'

38

Phillipa looked a little surprised.

'You told me, Mrs Haymes, that this man, Rudi Scherz, was quite unknown to you? That when you saw him there, dead, it was the first time you had seen him. Is that right?'

'Certainly. I had never seen him before.'

'You did not, for example, have a conversation with him in the summerhouse of Little Paddocks?'

'In the *summerhouse*?'

He was almost sure he heard a note of fear in her voice.

'Yes, Mrs Haymes. I am told that you had a conversation with this man, Rudi Scherz, and that he asked you where he could hide. You replied that you would show him – and the time, a quarter-past six, was definitely mentioned.'

There was a moment's silence. Then Phillipa laughed.

'I don't know who told you that,' she said. 'But I can guess. It's a very silly story. For some reason, Mitzi dislikes me.'

'So it's not true?'

'Of course it's not true … I never met or saw Rudi Scherz in my life, and I was nowhere near the house that morning. I was over here, working.'

Inspector Craddock said, very gently, 'Which morning?'

'Every morning. I'm here every morning.' She added, 'It's no good listening to what Mitzi tells you. Everyone knows that she tells lies all the time.'

♦

Later, Craddock was talking to Sergeant Fletcher.

'So there are two young women with different stories,' he said. 'Which one should I believe?'

'Everyone agrees that this foreign girl tells lies,' said Sergeant Fletcher. 'So if I were you, I would believe Mrs Haymes.'

Craddock remembered Phillipa Haymes's steady blue eyes and the way she had said *that morning* very quickly. But he had not told her whether the conversation in the summerhouse had taken place in the morning or the afternoon.

And there had been fear in Phillipa's voice as she asked: 'In the *summerhouse*?'

He decided to keep an open mind on the subject.

♦

Inspector Craddock went to see Miss Marple while she was staying with Bunch Harmon at the vicarage for a few days. They sat outside in the garden. But although it was sunny and peaceful, Inspector Craddock felt afraid – afraid for Miss Marple.

'Don't go around asking too many questions,' he said suddenly. 'I've a feeling – I have really – that it isn't *safe*.'

Miss Marple smiled a little.

'But we old women always ask questions,' she said. 'If we ask questions, it helps us to find out if people are who they say they are. Because that's what's worrying you, isn't it? The world has changed so much since the war. Fifteen years ago, everyone in a village like Chipping Cleghorn knew who everyone else was. But now every village is full of people who have just moved there. And you only know about them from what they tell you. But nobody *knows* any more who anyone really is.'

And that, thought Craddock, was exactly what was troubling him. He didn't know. Because of the oiled door, Craddock knew that somebody in Letitia Blacklock's sitting-room was not the pleasant friendly country neighbour he or she pretended to be.

And because of that, he was afraid for Miss Marple, who was old and weak and who noticed things. He could check all Miss Blacklock's relatives and neighbours, but it would take time. And he didn't have time, because Belle Goedler was dying.

He felt very worried, and told Miss Marple about Randall Goedler and about Pip and Emma.

'Perhaps they don't exist,' he said. 'Perhaps they're living in

Europe somewhere. On the other hand, one of them may be here in Chipping Cleghorn. They're about twenty-five years old, those cousins of hers … I wonder when she saw them last –'

Miss Marple said gently, 'I'll find out for you, shall I? It will be quite simple, Inspector, you really need not worry.'

Pip and Emma, thought Craddock, Pip and Emma. That attractive young man, the girl with the cool stare …

He said, 'I may find out something more about them in the next forty-eight hours. I'm going up to Scotland to see Mrs Goedler. She may know a lot more about them.'

'Good,' said Miss Marple. 'I hope you've warned Miss Blacklock to be careful?'

'I've warned her, yes. And remember … I've warned you.'

'I can take care of myself, Inspector,' said Miss Marple.

♦

Mrs Harmon took Miss Marple to tea at Miss Blacklock's house.

'Hold-ups must be very, very frightening,' said Miss Marple. 'How did the burglar get in?'

'Well, I'm afraid we don't lock our doors much.'

'Oh, Letty!' cried Miss Bunner. 'I forgot to tell you. The Inspector opened the second sitting-room door this morning – the one that's never been opened – the one over there. He hunted for the key and said the door had been oiled.'

She paused, her mouth open. Miss Blacklock had been signalling to her to be quiet, but it was too late.

'Oh, Lotty, I'm so – sorry – I mean, oh, I'm so sorry, Letty – oh, dear, how stupid I am.'

'It doesn't matter,' said Miss Blacklock, but she was annoyed. 'But Inspector Craddock probably doesn't want that to be talked about. You do understand, don't you, Mrs Harmon?'

'Oh, yes,' said Bunch. 'We won't say anything, will we, Aunt Jane. But I wonder why he – Oh! I know! Of course, if that door could open too, perhaps someone went out of there in the dark and did the hold-up. But of course they didn't – because it was the man from the Royal Spa Hotel. Or wasn't it? … No, I don't understand at all.'

'Did it all happen in this room, then?' asked Miss Marple.

At once Dora Bunner and Bunch started to tell her about the shooting. Then Patrick came in and good-naturedly joined in the story. He even acted out the part of Rudi Scherz.

'And Aunt Letty was there – in the corner by the small table … Go and stand there, Aunt Letty.'

Miss Blacklock obeyed, and then Miss Marple was shown the actual bullet holes.

'I was just going to offer my guests cigarettes – ' Miss Blacklock pointed to the big silver cigarette-box on the table.

'That's a lovely table,' said Miss Marple politely. 'And what a very pretty lamp on it.'

'Isn't it delightful? There's a pair of them. The other's in the spare bedroom, I think.'

'I *do* like nice things,' said Miss Marple. 'So many *memories*. In photographs too, of course. I like to keep all the pictures of my nephews and nieces as babies – and then as children – and adults. I expect your aunt has many photographs of you,' she said, turning to Patrick.

'Oh, we're only cousins,' said Patrick. 'We're not close.'

'I believe your mother did send me one of you as a baby, Pat,' said Miss Blacklock. 'But I'm afraid I didn't keep it.'

'These days one often doesn't know one's younger relations at all,' said Miss Marple.

'You've got a wonderful book of old photos,' said Julia. 'Do you remember, Aunt Letty, we looked through it the other day. The hats were so funny!'

'Never mind, Aunt Letty,' said Patrick. 'In thirty years' time, Julia will look at photos of herself and think *they're* funny.'

♦

'Did you do that deliberately?' asked Bunch, as she and Miss Marple were walking home. 'Talk about photographs, I mean?'

'Well, my dear, it *is* interesting to know that Miss Blacklock didn't know either of her two young relatives by sight … Yes – I think Inspector Craddock will be interested to hear that.'

Chapter 7   Morning Activities in Chipping Cleghorn

Edmund Swettenham went to see Phillipa Haymes as she was working as usual in the gardens at Dayas Hall.

'Please go away, Edmund,' said Phillipa. 'You've no business to come here. Mrs Lucas won't like it.'

'You're wrong,' said Edmund. 'I *have* got business here. My mother has sent me with a pot of honey for Mrs Lucas.' He took a pot of honey out of his pocket. Then he said, 'What happens in your head, Phillipa? What do you think? What do you *feel*?'

Phillipa said quietly, 'My feelings are my own business.'

'They're mine too. I've a right to know. I didn't *want* to fall in love with you. I wanted to sit quietly and write my book. Tell me things. Is it your husband? Do you still love him? You're young – and you're extremely lovely – and I love you a lot. So tell me about your husband.'

'There's nothing to tell. We met and got married. Harry was born. Then Ronald went abroad. He – he was killed in Italy. And now there's Harry.'

'I like Harry,' said Edmund. 'He's a really nice boy. He likes me. Shall we get married, Phillipa? Will you try it?'

Phillipa looked at him. She saw a tall, rather serious young man with a worried face and large glasses.

'No,' said Phillipa. 'Definitely no. You don't know anything about me. In fact, you don't know anything about anyone.'

♦

Sergeant Fletcher was alone in the house at Little Paddocks.

It was Mitzi's free day. She always caught the eleven o'clock bus into Medenham Wells. By arrangement with Miss Blacklock, Sergeant Fletcher was alone in the house. Miss Blacklock had taken Dora Bunner down to the village. Fletcher worked fast. He had to find out who had oiled and prepared that door.

Mitzi hadn't been in the sitting-room, so she hadn't needed to use the door. Nor, thought Fletcher, had the neighbours, and they hadn't had the opportunity to oil and prepare the door. Sergeant Fletcher searched the bedrooms, but he couldn't find anything interesting. Suddenly he heard a sound downstairs. He went to the top of the stairs and looked down.

Mrs Swettenham was crossing the hall. She had a basket on her arm. She looked into the sitting-room, crossed the hall and went into the dining-room. Then she came out again without the basket.

Fletcher made a sound and Mrs Swettenham looked up.

'Is that you, Miss Blacklock?'

'No, Mrs Swettenham, it's me – Sergeant Fletcher.' He came downstairs. 'This house doesn't seem very well protected against burglars. Can anybody always walk in when they want to?'

'I just brought some apples for Miss Blacklock,' explained Mrs Swettenham. 'We all walk in and out of each other's houses, Sergeant. Nobody thinks about locking a door until it's dark.'

Fletcher felt shocked. He had supposed – wrongly – that someone in the house had oiled the door. But someone from outside could do it too. They only had to wait until Mitzi, Letitia Blacklock and Dora Bunner were out of the house.

That meant that anyone in the sitting-room that night could be the criminal.

◆

'Amy!' said Miss Hinchcliffe. 'I've been thinking about the other evening at Little Paddocks.'

'Really, Hinch?' asked Amy Murgatroyd.

'Yes. Take this spoon, Amy. Pretend it's a gun. Don't be nervous. Now come to the kitchen door. You're going to pretend to be the burglar. You stand *here*. Now you're going to hold up a lot of silly people. Take this torch. Switch it on.'

Miss Murgatroyd obediently raised her torch, waved her spoon and went towards the kitchen door. She changed the torch to her right hand, quickly turned the handle and stepped forward. She then changed the torch back to her left hand.

'But Hinch,' she said. 'The door is a swing door. It keeps closing on me, and I've got both hands full. I can't hold it open.'

'Exactly,' said Miss Hinchcliffe. 'The sitting-room door at Little Paddocks swings shut too. So how could the burglar hold a gun and a torch and keep the door open at the same time?'

◆

'It's a most extraordinary thing,' said Colonel Easterbrook to himself. 'Most extraordinary. Laura, do you remember that I showed you my gun? It was in this drawer, wasn't it?'

'Oh yes, Archie, a nasty horrible black thing.'

'Well, it's not there now. You haven't moved it?'

'How *extraordinary*! No, I'd never dare to touch it.'

'What about the cleaning woman – Mrs Butt?'

'Mrs Butt would never do a thing like that. Shall I ask her?'

'No – no, you'd better not. I don't want to start a lot of talk. Tell me, do you remember when I showed it to you?'

'Oh, about a week ago. I remember *quite* clearly. It was Saturday the 30th. The day after the hold-up at Miss Blacklock's.'

'Oh, good,' said Colonel Easterbrook. 'If my gun had

disappeared before the shooting – well, maybe that Swiss man stole it. But if you definitely remember seeing it *after* the hold-up – well, the gun he used wasn't mine, was it?'

'Perhaps Mrs Butt did take it,' said his wife. 'Perhaps she felt nervous after the hold-up and thought she'd like to – to have a gun in the house. But I can't possibly ask her. She might get upset and leave. And what would we do then? This is such a big house – I couldn't possibly clean it myself.'

'Of course not,' said the Colonel. 'Don't say anything.'

♦

Miss Marple came out of the vicarage gate and walked down a little path that led to the main street. She passed the pub, and the butcher's, and stopped to look in the window of a shop that sold old pictures. Suddenly she saw Dora Bunner going into the Bluebird Café. At once Miss Marple decided that she needed a cup of coffee. She pushed open the door of the café and went in.

'Oh, good morning, Miss Marple,' said Dora Bunner. 'Do sit down here. I'm quite alone.'

Miss Marple sat down in a blue armchair, and she and Dora Bunner started to chat about the weather. A bored-looking waitress came and took their order for coffee and cakes.

'I met a very pretty girl as we were leaving Miss Blacklock's house the other day,' said Miss Marple. 'She said she does gardening.'

'Oh, yes, Phillipa Haymes,' said Miss Bunner. 'Such a nice, quiet girl. A *lady*, if you know what I mean. She's a widow. Her husband was killed in Italy.'

'I wondered, perhaps, if there might be a little romance?' asked Miss Marple. 'With that tall young man with the glasses?'

'Oh, Edmund Swettenham. You think he admires her? He's such a strange young man. He's supposed to be *clever*.'

The bored-looking waitress brought their coffee.

'I was so interested to hear you were at school with Miss

Blacklock,' said Miss Marple. 'You are such old friends.'

'Yes.' Miss Bunner sighed. 'Few people would be as loyal to their friends as dear Miss Blacklock is. Those days seem so long ago. She was such a pretty, light-hearted girl and enjoyed life so much. It all seemed so sad.'

'Life can be hard,' said Miss Marple, although she had no idea what had seemed so sad.

'*Sad illness bravely suffered.* I always think of that poem. True courage and patience. *Nothing* is too good for dear Miss Blacklock. She deserves whatever good things come to her.'

'Money,' said Miss Marple, 'can make one's life much easier.'

'Money!' cried Miss Bunner. 'Most people can't imagine what it's like not to have money. They don't know what it's like to be really hungry. And trying to get a job – and being told you're too old. And you've *got* to pay your rent – or you're out in the street.

'I wrote to Letty. I saw her name in the paper. Miss Letitia Blacklock. I hadn't heard of her for years. She'd been secretary, you know, to that very rich man, Goedler. She was always a clever girl – the kind to do well – not because of her looks, but her character. And I thought – well, I thought – perhaps she'll remember me – and she's one of the people I could ask for a little help. I mean, she knew me – I'd been at school with – well, she knew me.' Tears came into Dora Bunner's eyes. 'And then Lotty came and took me away – said she needed someone to help her. How kind she was – how *sympathetic.* I'd do anything for her. I try very hard, but sometimes I make mistakes and say foolish things. But she's very patient. She always pretends that I am useful to her. That's real kindness.'

Miss Marple said gently, 'Yes, that's real kindness.'

'I used to worry about what would happen to me if something happened to Miss Blacklock. But one day she told me she'd left me some money in her will – and all her beautiful furniture.

'I'm not really as stupid as I look,' continued Miss Bunner.

'Miss Blacklock is too trusting. That Patrick! Twice, he's got into debt and got money out of her. She's too generous to him.'

'He's such a handsome young man,' said Miss Marple.

'He's too fond of making fun of people,' said Dora. 'I'm sure he was involved in that terrible shooting. I think he knew that young man. And I'm worried about that door – the detective saying it had been oiled. Because you see, I saw –'

'Most difficult for you,' said Miss Marple sympathetically. 'You don't want to criticise anyone to the police.'

'That's right!' cried Dora Bunner. 'You see, I found Patrick in the garden the other day. Patrick was there, holding a feather and an oily cup. And he jumped most guiltily when he saw me and said, "I was just wondering what this was doing here." But how did he find a thing like that, unless he was looking for it?

'And if you ask me, I believe that Patrick changed something about that lamp in the sitting-room – to make the lights go out – because I remember clearly that it was the shepherdess lamp – *not* the shepherd. And the next day –'

She stopped suddenly. Miss Marple turned and saw Miss Blacklock standing behind them.

'Coffee and chat, Bunny?' said Miss Blacklock sharply. 'Good morning, Miss Marple. Cold, isn't it?'

The door of the café opened and Bunch Harmon rushed in.

'Hello,' she said, 'am I too late for coffee?'

'No, dear,' said Miss Marple. 'Sit down and have a cup.'

'We must get home,' said Miss Blacklock to Dora. 'Have you done your shopping?' Her voice was friendly again.

'Yes, thank you, Letty. I just need to buy some aspirin.'

When Miss Blacklock and Miss Bunner had left, Bunch asked, 'What were you talking about?'

Miss Marple did not reply at once. Then she said, 'I was just thinking that people are very like each other.'

'Who are you thinking about, Aunt Jane?' asked Bunch.

'People in St Mary Mead?'

'Mostly … I was really thinking about Nurse Ellerton – really an excellent, kind woman. She took care of an old lady – seemed really fond of her. Then the old lady died. And another came and *she died*. Nurse Ellerton had poisoned them. They hadn't had long to live, she said, and one of them was in a lot of pain.'

'So she killed them out of kindness?'

'No, no. They had left her a lot of money. She liked money, you know. And then there was that young man – Mrs Pusey at the newspaper shop's nephew. He brought home stolen things. And then when the police came to the house and started asking questions, he tried to hit her on the head, so she couldn't tell them about him … Not a nice young man, but very good-looking. And then there was Mrs Cray at the wool shop. She loved her son, but he had some bad friends.'

'Anybody else?' asked Bunch.

'That girl at St Jean de Collines that summer. A very quiet girl. Everybody liked her, but they never found out much about her. We heard afterwards that her husband was a criminal – it made her feel different from other people. It made her, in the end, a little peculiar. There was also Mr Hodgson, the bank manager, who went on holiday and married a woman who was young enough to be his daughter. He didn't know anything about her except what she told him. And that definitely wasn't true.'

'Well,' said Bunch. 'You've described Dora Bunner, handsome Patrick, Mrs Swettenham and Edmund, and Phillipa Haymes and Colonel Easterbrook and his wife. Do you think you know who was responsible for the murder?'

'I don't know,' said Miss Marple. 'I got an idea for a moment – but it's gone. I wish I did know. There isn't very much time. That old lady up in Scotland may die very soon.'

'Then you really do believe in Pip and Emma,' said Bunch, staring. 'You think it was them – and that they'll try again?'

'Of course they'll try again,' said Miss Marple.

'But if it's Pip and Emma,' said Bunch, 'there are only two people it could be. It must be Patrick and Julia. They're brother and sister and they're the only ones who are the right age.'

'My dear, it isn't as simple as that. It could be Pip's wife if he's married, or Emma's husband. It could be their mother. And then there's their father. He wasn't a very nice man. Perhaps he could act the part of – of the Colonel, for example. I think a lot of money is involved. And I'm afraid that people will do terrible things to get their hands on a lot of money.'

Chapter 8   Memories of the Past

Inspector Craddock took the night train to Scotland. A car was waiting to meet him, and took him to Belle Goedler's house. He was served breakfast, and then a tall, middle-aged woman in a nurse's uniform came in. She introduced herself as Sister McClelland.

'Mrs Goedler is ready to see you,' she said. 'I'd better warn you about what will happen. She will talk and enjoy talking and then – quite suddenly – she will become very tired. In preparation for your visit, I've given her a drug to keep her awake. When she gets tired, send for me.'

'How exactly is Mrs Goedler's health?' asked Craddock.

'She's dying. She only has a few more weeks to live.'

Craddock was shown into a large bedroom where a fire was burning. An old lady lay in a bed. There were lines of pain on her face, but also lines of sweetness. And there was, Craddock noticed, a surprisingly playful look in her blue eyes.

'Well,' she said 'it's not often that I receive a visit from the police. I hear Letitia Blacklock wasn't much hurt by the attempt to take her life. How is my dear Blackie? It's a long time since I've seen her … I suppose you want to ask about the money?'

'Why did your husband leave his money like that?'

'You mean, why did he leave it to Blackie? Not for the reason you've probably been thinking.' The playful look in Mrs Goedler's eyes grew brighter. 'Randall was never in love with her, and she wasn't with him. I think Randall thought of Blackie as a kind of younger brother. He depended on her judgement, which was always excellent. Letitia Blacklock would never do anything that was dishonest. She's a very fine character. I've always admired her. Her sister was an invalid. She never saw people or went out. So when the girls' father died, Letitia gave up her job to go home and look after her. Randall was angry, but it made no difference.'

'How long was that before your husband died?'

'A couple of years, I think. Randall made his will before she left the company, and he didn't change it. He said to me, "We've no one of our own."'

'But that's not quite true, is it, Mrs Goedler?' said Craddock. 'He had a sister.'

'Oh, Sonia. But they quarrelled years ago. He didn't like the man she married – Dmitri Stamfordis. Randall said he was a criminal. But Sonia was madly in love with him.'

'And Randall and Sonia never made up their quarrel?'

'No. She was angry because he had tried to prevent the marriage. But I got a letter from her about eighteen months afterwards. She wrote from Budapest. She told me to tell Randall that she was extremely happy and that she'd just had twins. She intended to call them Pip and Emma. Then she went right out of our lives. But I persuaded Randall to put Pip and Emma's names into his will if Blackie had an accident and died before me. He wasn't happy about it, but he did do that.'

'And since then,' Craddock said slowly, 'you've heard nothing of Sonia or her children?'

'Nothing – they may be dead – they may be – anywhere.'

They might be in Chipping Cleghorn, thought Craddock.

51

Suddenly a look of fear came into Belle Goedler's eyes. She said, 'Don't let them hurt Blackie … You must look after Blackie … ' Her voice went quiet.

Later Craddock asked Sister McClelland, 'Does Mrs Goedler have any old photographs?'

'I'm afraid there's nothing,' said the nurse. 'All her personal papers and furniture were burned in a fire during the war.'

So that was that, Craddock thought. But he felt his journey to Scotland had not been a waste of time. He had made some progress with the case.

'Sonia Goedler was a rich woman when she got married, but perhaps things changed,' he thought. 'Perhaps Pip and Emma came to England and learned about the contents of their uncle's will, and about Miss Letitia Blacklock. Then they found out about Randall Goedler's widow. She's an invalid, living up in Scotland, and she hasn't long to live. *If Letitia Blacklock dies before her*, they will get a lot of money. They'd find out where Letitia Blacklock is living. And they'd go there – but not as themselves … I'm sure that Pip, or Emma, or both of them, are in Chipping Cleghorn now.'

♦

In the kitchen at Little Paddocks, Miss Blacklock was giving instructions to Mitzi.

'It's Miss Bunner's birthday, and some people will be coming to tea. I want you to make some nice sandwiches and that special chocolate cake of yours.'

'You mean the rich one?' asked Mitzi. She smiled. 'Delicious, these English people will say – delicious … ' Suddenly her face grew sad. 'Mr Patrick called it Delicious Death. My cake!'

'He only meant,' said Miss Blacklock, 'that it was worth dying to eat such a cake.'

'Well, I do not like that word – *death*. They are not dying because they eat my cake – no, they feel much, much better …'

Miss Blacklock left the kitchen. Dora Bunner was outside.

'Edmund Swettenham just phoned,' she said. 'He wished me a happy birthday and said he was bringing me a pot of honey as a present. And Miss Hinchcliffe is bringing some eggs.'

'And there's a lovely box of chocolates from Julia,' said Miss Blacklock. 'Let's go and feed the hens.'

♦

'What do I see in front of me?' cried Patrick excitedly as everyone sat down around the dining-room table. '*Delicious Death.*'

'Shh!' said Miss Blacklock. 'Don't let Mitzi hear you. She doesn't like you calling her cake by that name.'

'But it *is* Delicious Death. Is it Bunny's birthday cake?'

'Yes, it is,' said Miss Bunner. 'I really am having the most wonderful birthday.' Her cheeks were red with excitement.

Everyone ate the good things on the tea table.

'I feel slightly sick,' said Julia as they got up. 'It's that cake. I remember I felt just the same last time. It's so rich.'

'Have you got a new gardener?' asked Miss Hinchcliffe as they returned to the sitting-room. 'I saw a man near the henhouse.'

'That's our detective,' said Julia. 'He's protecting Aunt Letty.'

'But surely it's all finished now,' cried Mrs Easterbrook.

'No,' said Edmund Swettenham. 'Someone wants to murder her at the first opportunity.'

'Oh, don't say that, Mr Swettenham.' Dora Bunner began to cry. 'I'm sure nobody here could want to kill dear, dear Letty.'

'It was just a joke,' said Edmund hurriedly, turning red.

'Shall we listen to the six o'clock news?' asked Phillipa.

Patrick whispered to Julia, 'We need Mrs Harmon here. She would be sure to say in that high voice, "I suppose somebody *is* still waiting for the chance to murder you, Miss Blacklock?"'

'I'm glad she and Miss Marple couldn't come,' said Julia. 'That old woman can't keep her nose out of other people's business.'

After the guests had gone home, Miss Blacklock said, 'Did you enjoy yourself, Bunny?'

'Oh, I did. But I've got a terrible headache. I'll go and lie down, I think. I'll take a couple of aspirins and have a nice sleep.'

A few minutes later, Dora came downstairs again.

'I can't find my aspirin,' she said.

'Well, take some of mine, dear,' said Miss Blacklock. 'They're by my bed.' Miss Bunner went upstairs again. 'She's had a lot of excitement today, and it isn't good for her,' said Miss Blacklock. 'But I really think she's enjoyed herself!'

♦

'Phillipa, my dear, I want to talk to you,' said Miss Blacklock when they were alone.

'Yes, Miss Blacklock?' Phillipa looked up in slight surprise.

'I've noticed that you've looked worried recently. I know you get anxious sometimes about your boy's education. That's why I want to tell you something. I drove into Milchester this afternoon to see my lawyer. I thought I'd like to make a new will. Apart from what I'm leaving to Bunny, everything goes to you.'

'What?' Phillipa turned round quickly. Her eyes stared. 'But I don't want it – really, I don't … Why to *me*?'

'Perhaps,' said Miss Blacklock, 'because there's no one else.'

'But there's Patrick and Julia. They're your relations.'

'Yes, there's Patrick and Julia.' There was a strange note in Miss Blacklock's voice. 'But they're not close relations. They have no claim on me. I've become fond of you, Phillipa – and there's the boy … You won't get very much if I die now – but in a few weeks time it might be different.'

Her eyes met Phillipa's steadily.

'But you're not going to die!' cried Phillipa.

'Not if I can avoid it by being careful,' said Miss Blacklock.

She left the room quickly. Phillipa heard her speaking to Julia in the hall. Then Julia came into the sitting-room. There was a cold, unfriendly look in her eyes.

'You've done very well for yourself, haven't you, Phillipa?'

'So you heard –?'

'Yes. I think that I was meant to hear. Our Letty's no fool … Well, if anyone murders her now, you'll be the main suspect.'

'But it would be stupid to kill her now when – if I waited –'

'So you do know about old Mrs What's-her-name dying up in Scotland?'

'I don't want to take anything away from you and Patrick.'

'Don't you, my dear? I'm sorry – but I don't believe you.'

♦

When Inspector Craddock got back to Milchester, he went to make his report to Rydesdale. Rydesdale listened carefully.

'Patrick and Julia are the right age to be Pip and Emma, sir,' said Craddock.

'Yes, but we've been checking their stories,' said Rydesdale. 'Patrick was in the Navy and his record there is real. We've also asked their mother, Mrs Simmons, who lives in France. She says that of course her son and daughter are at Chipping Cleghorn with her cousin Letitia Blacklock.'

'And Mrs Simmons *is* Mrs Simmons?'

'She's been Mrs Simmons for a very long time.'

The Chief Constable handed a piece of paper to Craddock.

'Here's something we've found out about Mrs Easterbrook.'

The Inspector read the paper with interest.

'Well,' he said, 'she's completely deceived that old fool, her husband. But it has no relationship with this business.'

'No. And here's something that concerns Mrs Haymes.'

Again, Craddock read it with interest.

'I think I'll have another talk with the lady,' he said.

'You think this information may be important?' said Rydesdale.

'I think it might be.' The two men were silent for a moment. Then Craddock asked, 'What has Sergeant Fletcher been doing, sir?'

'Fletcher has been extremely active. He searched the house by agreement with Miss Blacklock, but he didn't find anything important. Then he's been thinking about who had the chance to oil that door when that foreign girl was out.'

'Who do we know was in the house when it was empty?'

'Almost everyone. Miss Murgatroyd brought a hen. Mrs Swettenham came to fetch some meat. Miss Hinchcliffe just called in. Mrs Easterbrook was taking her dogs for a walk and called to see Miss Blacklock. And the Colonel went there with a book on India that Miss Blacklock wanted to read. We don't know about Edmund Swettenham. He said he visited occasionally with messages from his mother.'

Rydesdale continued, with a slight smile, 'Miss Marple has also been active. Fletcher reports that she had morning coffee at the Bluebird Café. She's been to sherry with Miss Murgatroyd and Miss Hinchcliffe, and to tea at Little Paddocks. She's admired Mrs Swettenham's garden, and looked at Colonel Easterbrook's souvenirs from India.'

'She may be able to tell us if Colonel Easterbrook is a real colonel or not.'

'She'd know – I agree. He seems all right. But we'd have to check with the Indian officials.'

'We need to act quickly, sir,' said Craddock. 'Mrs Goedler is a dying woman. That means our murderer can't afford to wait. And there's another thing. He – or she – must know we're checking everybody.'

'And that takes time,' said Rydesdale with a sigh.

'So that's another reason for hurry. If Belle Goedler dies –'

He stopped as a constable entered.

'There's a phone call from Constable Legg from Chipping Cleghorn,' the constable said.

'Put him through,' said Rydesdale. He picked up the phone and his face grew very serious as he listened. He put the phone down. 'It's Dora Bunner,' he said. 'She wanted some aspirin. She took some from a bottle beside Letitia Blacklock's bed. There were only a few pills left in the bottle. She took two and left one. The doctor's got that one and is sending it to be examined. He says it's definitely *not* aspirin.'

'She's dead?'

'Yes. She was found dead in her bed this morning. She died in her sleep, the doctor says. He thinks she was poisoned.'

'Aspirin pills by Letitia Blacklock's bed,' said Craddock. 'The clever, clever devil. Patrick told me that Miss Blacklock threw away a half bottle of sherry and opened a new one. She probably didn't think of doing that with an open bottle of aspirin. Who was in the house this time – within the last day or two?'

Rydesdale looked at him.

'Everybody was there yesterday,' he said. 'There was a birthday party for Miss Bunner.'

♦

Miss Marple was waiting for Miss Blacklock in the sitting-room at Little Paddocks. She had brought a note from Reverend Harmon about the arrangements for Dora Bunner's funeral. She looked around and thought about what Dora Bunner had said in the Bluebird Café. Dora had said that Patrick had changed something on the lamp to make the lights go out.

What lamp? And how had he changed it? She probably, Miss Marple decided, meant the small lamp on the table by the wall. It was a figure of a shepherd which had been a candle-holder but had been made into an electric lamp. What had Dora Bunner said? 'I remember clearly that it was the shepherdess lamp. And the next day – ' Certainly it was a shepherd now.

Miss Marple remembered that when she and Bunch had

57

come to tea, Dora Bunner had said that the lamp was one of a *pair*. Of course – a shepherd and a shepherdess. It had been the shepherdess on the day of the hold-up – and the next day it had been the *other* lamp, the shepherd. And Dora Bunner thought that Patrick had changed them. Why?

Miss Marple looked at the lamp in front of her. The flex ran along the table, then down over the edge of the table to the wall. There was a small switch half-way along the flex.

Patrick Simmons … a handsome young man, who young and older women liked. Could Patrick Simmons be 'Pip'?

The door opened and Miss Blacklock came in. She looked, thought Miss Marple, many years older. All the life and energy had gone out of her.

'I'm very sorry, interrupting you like this,' said Miss Marple. 'I've brought you a note from Reverend Harmon.'

She held it out and Miss Blacklock took it and opened it.

'Reverend Harmon is a very understanding man,' she said quietly. Her voice broke suddenly and she started to cry.

Miss Marple sat quietly.

Miss Blacklock sat up at last. Her face was wet with tears.

'I'm sorry,' she said. 'She was the only connection with the past, you see. The only one who – who *remembered*. Now that she's gone, I'm quite alone.'

'I know what you mean,' said Miss Marple. 'I have nephews and nieces and kind friends – but there's no one who knew me as a young girl. I've been alone for quite a long time now.'

There was the sound of a man's voice in the hall.

'That's Inspector Craddock,' said Miss Blacklock.

Craddock came in. When he saw Miss Marple, he did not look happy at all.

'Oh,' he said. 'So *you're* here.'

'I am going at once – at once,' said Miss Marple. 'Please don't let me be in your way.' She left the room.

'We've got to work fast,' Craddock said to Miss Blacklock. 'I've checked with Mrs Goedler. There are only a few people who would become rich from your death. First, Pip and Emma. Tell me, would you recognise Sonia Goedler if you saw her?'

'Recognise Sonia? Of course –' She stopped suddenly. 'No,' she said slowly, 'perhaps I wouldn't. It's been a long time. Thirty years … She'd be an old woman now.'

'What was she like when you remember her?'

'Sonia?' Miss Blacklock thought for some moments. 'She was rather small, dark …'

'Tell me, do you think it's possible that Mrs Swettenham might be Sonia Goedler? Or Miss Hinchcliffe or Miss Murgatroyd?'

'*Mrs Swettenham*?' Miss Blacklock looked at him in surprise. 'Oh, no, that's impossible. And Miss Hinchcliffe is too tall. And I'm sure Miss Murgatroyd couldn't be Sonia.'

'I'd like to see a photo of Sonia Goedler.'

'Very well,' said Miss Blacklock. 'Let me see. I was tidying a lot of books in the cupboard. Julia was helping me. There were some old books of photographs there. Where did we put them? Perhaps Julia will remember. She's at home today.'

The Inspector found Julia in a passage upstairs. She had just come out of a door with some stairs going up behind it.

'I was up in the attic,' she explained. 'What is it?'

Inspector Craddock told her about the books of photographs.

'We put them in the big cupboard in the study, I think.'

She led the way downstairs and pushed open the study door. Near the window there was a large cupboard. Julia pulled it open. The Inspector took a couple of old-fashioned books of photographs from the bottom shelf.

Miss Blacklock came in. Craddock put the books on the table and turned the pages. He saw pictures of women in large old-fashioned hats. The photos had old writing underneath them.

'The photographs would be in this book,' said Miss Blacklock.

'On the second or third page.' She turned a page and stopped.

There were several empty spaces on the page. Craddock bent down and read the writing. 'Sonia … Self … Charlotte … R.G.'

'Sonia and Belle on the beach.'

'There weren't any empty spaces when we looked at them the other day,' said Miss Blacklock, 'were there, Julia?'

'I didn't look very closely – only at some of the dresses. But no … you're right, Aunt Letty, there weren't any empty spaces.'

Craddock stood up. 'Somebody,' he said, 'has removed every photograph of Sonia Goedler from this book.'

Chapter 9   Miss Murgatroyd Remembers

Inspector Craddock went to see Phillipa Haymes again.

'I think you told me, Mrs Haymes, that your husband was killed fighting in Italy? Wouldn't it have been better if you had told me the truth – that he ran away from the army?'

Craddock saw Phillipa's face grow white, and her hands close tightly and open again.

'Do you have to find out about everything?' she asked.

'We expect people to tell us the truth about themselves,' said Craddock. 'When did you see him last, Mrs Haymes?'

'I haven't seen him for years.'

'Are you sure that's true? I think you saw him about a fortnight ago. It never seemed to me very likely that you met Rudi Scherz in the summerhouse. I suggest, Mrs Haymes, that the man you came back from work to meet that morning was your husband.'

'I didn't meet anybody in the summerhouse.'

'Perhaps he didn't have any money, and you gave him some? Men who run away from the army are often rather desperate. They often take part in robberies, you know. *And they often have guns that they've brought back from abroad.* '

'I haven't seen him,' said Phillipa Haymes again.

Craddock felt angry and confused. He was sure that she was lying. Then, suddenly, he wondered what Julia had been doing in the attic. He ran quickly upstairs and climbed the narrow stairs that led up to the attic.

There were boxes and old suitcases in the attic, and a small case with papers and letters inside. The initials C.L.B. were on the outside of the case. He supposed it had belonged to Letitia's sister Charlotte. The letters were old and yellow. He took one out and looked at it. The letter began *Dearest Charlotte* and was signed *Your loving sister, Letitia*.

Craddock felt excited. These letters which Letitia had written to her sister might contain a clue. They created a true picture of the past. Perhaps there was also a photo of Sonia Goedler. He packed the letters up again, closed the case and went downstairs. Letitia Blacklock was waiting for him at the bottom of the stairs.

'Miss Blacklock,' said Craddock, 'I've found some letters here, written by you to your sister Charlotte many years ago. May I take them away and read them? They might give a picture of Sonia Goedler's character – a clue – that will help.'

'They're private letters, Inspector,' said Miss Blacklock angrily. 'Take them! But you'll find very little about Sonia.'

'We've got to try everything. The danger is very real.'

Miss Blacklock said, biting her lips, 'I know. Bunny was killed by an aspirin that was meant for me. It may be Patrick, or Julia, or Phillipa, or Mitzi next – somebody young with their life in front of them. Take the letters – and then burn them. They don't mean anything to anyone except me. Nobody remembers …'

Her hand went up to the choker of false pearls she was wearing. Craddock thought how strange it looked with her coat and skirt.

'Take the letters,' she said again.

♦

The next afternoon was dark and windy. Inspector Craddock took the letters to Miss Marple at the vicarage and explained how he had found them. Miss Marple had her chair pulled close to the fire. Bunch was there too.

'I'd like you to look at this letter,' said the Inspector.

Miss Marple took the letter. She unfolded it and read it. In the letter, Letitia Blacklock told Charlotte about Sonia Goedler's marriage to Dimitri Stamfordis. The last paragraph read:

Sonia asks to be remembered to you. She has just come in and is closing and unclosing her hands like an angry cat. I think she and Randall have had another quarrel. Of course Sonia can be very annoying. It's difficult to argue with that cool stare of hers.

Miss Marple folded the letter and handed it back.

'Well, what picture do you get of Sonia?' asked Craddock.

'It's difficult, you know, to see anyone through another person's mind,' said Miss Marple.

'*Closing and unclosing her hands like an angry cat,*' said Craddock. 'You know, that reminds me of someone … ' He thought hard for a moment. 'We've never found that gun, you know. It didn't belong to Rudi Scherz. If I knew who had a gun in Chipping Cleghorn – '

'Colonel Easterbrook has one,' said Bunch. 'Mrs Butt told me. She's my cleaning-woman. She cleans the Easterbrooks' house too. She told me about six months ago.'

'Colonel Easterbrook went up to Little Paddocks to leave a book there one day,' said Craddock. 'It wasn't impossible for him to oil that door. But I've stopped worrying about Pip and Emma. I'm concentrating on Sonia. I wish I knew what she looked like. There were one or two photos with these letters, but none of the photos was of her.'

'How do you know? Do you know what she looked like?'

'She was small and dark, Miss Blacklock said.'

'Really,' said Miss Marple, 'that's *very* interesting.'

'There was one photo that reminded me of someone. A tall

fair girl with her hair on top of her head. I don't know who she was, but it wasn't Sonia. I hoped there might be a photo of Dmitri Stamfordis – but there wasn't.'

The telephone rang. Bunch got up and went out into the hall. She came back a few moments later.

'It's for you, Inspector.'

Slightly surprised, the Inspector went out to the hall. He shut the door of the sitting-room carefully behind him.

'Craddock? Rydesdale here. I've been looking through your report about Phillipa Haymes. She states that she hasn't seen her husband since he ran away from the army.'

'Yes, sir,' said Craddock. 'But in my opinion she was lying.'

'I agree with you,' said Rydesdale. 'Do you remember that about ten days ago a man was hit by a lorry while he was saving a child? He was taken to Milchester Hospital and died yesterday. He was Captain Ronald Haymes.'

'Phillipa Haymes's husband?'

'Yes. He'd got an old Chipping Cleghorn bus ticket on him – and quite a lot of money.'

'So he *did* get money from his wife? I always thought he was the man Mitzi heard talking to Phillipa Haymes in the summerhouse. But surely, sir, that lorry accident was before –'

'Yes,' said Rydesdale. 'He was taken to Milchester Hospital on the 28th. The hold-up at Little Paddocks was on the 29th. So he didn't have any connection with it. But his wife doesn't know that. Perhaps she thought he was involved. That's why she kept quiet about him. He was her husband. It was a brave thing to do, wasn't it? Rescuing that child from the lorry? Yes, very brave. His son needn't be ashamed of him now. And the young woman will be able to marry again. You'd better go and tell her.'

Bunch Harmon was going out for the evening.

'I'll put a lamp beside you,' she said to Miss Marple. 'It's so dark in here. There's going to be a storm, I think.'

She lifted a small lamp to the other side of the table. As the flex pulled across the table, the Harmons' cat jumped up. It bit through the flex so violently that it became frayed.

'Bad cat!' said Bunch.

Miss Marple put out a hand to turn on the lamp.

'It doesn't turn on there. You have to press that switch half-way along the flex. Wait – let me take these flowers away.'

Bunch lifted a bowl of roses across the table. The cat knocked playfully against her arm and she spilled some of the water out of the vase. It fell on the frayed area of the flex. Miss Marple pressed the small switch on the flex. There was a flash and a small bang in the place where the water had made the frayed flex wet.

'Oh dear,' said Bunch. 'It's fused, and now I suppose all the lights in here are off.' She tried them. 'Yes, they are. It's all that cat's fault. Aunt Jane – what's the matter? Did it frighten you?'

'No. I've just realised something …'

'I'll go and fix the fuse and get another lamp.'

'No, dear, I don't want any more light. I just want to sit quietly and think about something. Hurry, dear, or you'll miss your bus.'

When Bunch had gone, Miss Marple sat quietly for about two minutes. Then she pulled a piece of paper towards her.

She wrote first: *Lamp*? and put a heavy line underneath it. After a time, she wrote another word, and then more notes.

♦

In the rather dark sitting-room of Boulders, Miss Hinchcliffe and Miss Murgatroyd were having an argument about the shooting.

'But Hinch, I can't remember anything,' said Miss Murgatroyd.

'Now listen, Amy Murgatroyd, we're going to think about this properly. You can't hold open a door, wave a torch and shoot with a gun all at the same time.'

'But he *did* have a gun,' said Miss Murgatroyd. 'I saw it. It was there on the floor beside him.'

'When he was dead, yes. But *he* didn't fire it.'

'Then who did?' asked Miss Murgatroyd.

'That's what we're going to find out. It was the same person who put a couple of poisoned aspirin pills by Letty Blacklock's bed. But let's go back to the attempt on Letty Blacklock. Now, think hard, and try and remember what you saw.'

'But I didn't see *anything*.'

'Use your brain, Amy,' said Miss Hinchcliffe. 'Where were you when the lights went out? You were behind the door. You were the only person who could see into the room. The rest of us couldn't see anything because the torch was shining into our eyes. But the door was between you and the torch.'

'But the torch was going round and round –'

'Showing you *what*? It rested on *faces*, didn't it?'

'Yes – yes, it did … I saw Miss Bunner and Mrs Harmon …'

'Good, Amy. Now, when you've thought about who you *did* see, we can get onto the important point – was there anyone you *didn't* see.'

Miss Murgatroyd shut her eyes. She said softly to herself, 'The flowers … on the big table … the big armchair … the torch didn't come round as far as you, Hinch – Mrs Harmon, yes …'

The telephone rang sharply. Miss Hinchcliffe went to answer it.

The obedient Miss Murgatroyd, her eyes closed, was remembering the night of the 29th. The torch, sweeping slowly round … a group of people … the windows … the sofa … Dora Bunner … the wall … the table with the lamp …

'But that's *extraordinary*!' said Miss Murgatroyd.

'What?' Miss Hinchcliffe was shouting angrily into the telephone. 'The dog's at the station? Since this morning?' She banged down the phone. 'Our dog's been at the station since this morning – with no water. I'm going to get her right away.'

She rushed out. Miss Murgatroyd followed, speaking excitedly.

'But, listen, Hinch, a most extraordinary thing … I don't understand it …'

Miss Hinchcliffe had run out of the door to the garage.

'We'll continue with this when I come back,' she called. 'I'm in a hurry now. I can't wait for you to come with me.'

She pressed the starter of the car and backed out of the garage.

'But listen, Hinch, I must tell you – '

The car moved quickly forwards. Miss Murgatroyd's voice followed it on a high, excited note.

'But, Hinch, *she wasn't there* …'

Chapter 10   Looking for Miss Marple

Dark storm clouds had been gathering in the sky. As Miss Murgatroyd stood looking after the car, the first big drops of rain began to fall. Miss Murgatroyd went out to the clothes line in the garden, where she had hung some blouses some hours before.

'Oh, dear – and they were nearly dry …'

She turned her head as she heard someone approaching. Then she smiled a pleased welcome.

'Hello – do go inside, you'll get wet.'

'Let me help you. Here's your scarf. It's fallen on the ground. Shall I put it round your neck?'

'Oh, thank you … Yes, perhaps …'

The woollen scarf was slipped round her neck and then, suddenly, pulled tight. Miss Murgatroyd's mouth opened, but no sound came out.

♦

On her way back from the station, Miss Hinchcliffe stopped the car to pick up Miss Marple, who was hurrying along the street.

'Hello!' she shouted. 'You'll get very wet. Come and have tea with us. Mind the dog. She's rather nervous.'

Miss Marple got in and Miss Hinchcliffe drove to Boulders. A crowd of eager hens surrounded the ladies as they got out.

'Why hasn't Amy given them their corn?' said Miss Hinchcliffe. She led Miss Marple into the cottage. 'Amy!'

A noise was coming from the garden.

'What's the matter with that dog?' said Miss Hinchcliffe. She went into the garden and Miss Marple followed. The dog was pushing its nose into something that was lying on the ground.

Miss Hinchcliffe walked across the grass and looked down. The face was blue and the tongue was sticking out.

Miss Marple put her arm around Miss Hinchcliffe.

'I'll kill whoever did this to Amy,' the younger woman said in a low, quiet voice, 'if I get my hands on her …'

'*Her*?' Miss Marple said questioningly.

'Yes. I think I know …'

She stood for another moment, looking down at her dear friend, and then turned towards the house. Her voice was dry and hard.

'We must ring the police,' she said. 'It's my fault that Amy's lying out there. I made a game of it … But murder isn't a game.'

She told Miss Marple about the conversation she and Amy had been having before she left to go to the station.

'She called after me, you know, just as I was leaving … That's how I know it's a woman and not a man … If only I'd *listened*! Perhaps *she* was outside there, then – yes, of course … coming to the house … and there were Amy and I shouting at each other. She heard it all …'

'You haven't told me what your friend said.'

'Just one sentence! "*She wasn't there.*"'

She paused. 'You see? One of those three women – Mrs

Swettenham, Mrs Easterbrook and Julia Simmons – wasn't there … She wasn't there in the sitting-room because she'd gone out through the other door and was in the hall.'

'Yes,' said Miss Marple. 'I see. Tell me … exactly how did Miss Murgatroyd say the words? Did she say "*She* wasn't there." or did she say, "She *wasn't* there." or "She wasn't *there*?"'

'I don't know.' Miss Hinchcliffe shook her head. 'I can't remember … Does it make any difference?'

'Yes,' said Miss Marple. 'It makes a lot of difference.'

♦

The postman brought two letters to Chipping Cleghorn that afternoon. One was addressed to Phillipa Haymes and was from her son, Harry. The second letter was for Miss Blacklock. It was written in an unfamiliar handwriting.

Dear Cousin Letty,

I hope it will be all right for me to come to you on Tuesday? I wrote to Patrick two days ago, but he hasn't answered.

My train arrives at Chipping Cleghorn at 6.15 if that's convenient?

With love,

Julia Simmons

Miss Blacklock read the letter with great surprise. Then she handed it to Phillipa.

'I'd like you to read this.'

Phillipa read it with a puzzled expression on her face. 'I don't understand.'

'Nor do I … Call Patrick and Julia.'

Phillipa went to the bottom of the stairs and called. Patrick came running down the stairs and entered the room.

'Hello, Aunt Letty,' he said cheerfully. 'Do you want me?'

'Yes, I do. Perhaps you'll give me an explanation of *this*?' asked Miss Blacklock. Patrick took the letter and read it.

'I meant to contact her, but I forgot. How stupid I am!'

'This letter, I suppose, is from your sister, Julia?'

'Yes – yes, it is.'

'*So who is the young woman who you brought here as Julia Simmons – who you said was your sister and my cousin?*'

'Well, I met her at a party. It seemed a good idea for her to come here. You see, the real Julia is mad about acting. She got a chance to join a theatre company up in Scotland. But Mother was very angry about the idea. We thought that if another girl came here, pretending to be Julia, Julia could go and join the theatre company. And Mother wouldn't find out that Julia wasn't here.'

'But who is this other young woman?' said Miss Blacklock.

Patrick turned as Julia came into the room.

'The game has ended,' he said. 'Aunt Letty knows everything.'

Julia looked surprised. Then she came forward and sat down.

'OK,' she said calmly. 'I suppose you're very angry?'

'*Who are you?*'

Julia sighed. 'I think the moment's come when I tell the truth. I'm one half of Pip and Emma. My name is Emma Jocelyn Stamfordis. My father is Dmitri Stamfordis. My father and mother separated about three years after Pip and I were born. Pip stayed with Mother, and Father took me. I've no idea what happened to him. I had a few adventures myself. In the war, I was with the French Resistance* for a time.

'After the war, I came to London. I knew that Mother's brother was a very rich man. I looked up his will to see if there was anything for me. There wasn't – not directly. I found out that you were going to inherit all his money after his widow died. I'll be quite honest. It seemed to me that if I got to know you in a friendly kind of way, and you liked me, perhaps you would take pity on me and let me have some money. Then, just by chance, I met Patrick at a party – and I

* French Resistance: an organisation that fought secretly against the Nazis when they controlled France in World War II

learned that he was your nephew or your cousin, or something. It was a wonderful opportunity. Patrick fell in love with me. The real Julia loved acting, so I persuaded her to join a theatre company.

'But when that hold-up happened, I knew I would be in trouble. I've got a very good motive for wanting to kill you. I thought I'd better continue pretending to be Julia. How could I know that the real Julia would decide to leave the theatre company? She writes to Patrick and asks if she can come here, but instead of telling her to keep away he forgets to contact her!'

She glanced angrily at Patrick and sighed.

'*Pip and Emma*,' said Miss Blacklock softly. 'I never believed they were real. You're Emma,' she said. 'Where's Pip?'

Julia looked into her eyes with an innocent stare.

'I don't know,' she said. 'I have no idea.'

'I think you're lying, Julia. When did you last see him?'

'I haven't seen him since we were both three years old,' said Julia clearly. 'That's when my mother took him away.'

'Julia,' said Miss Blacklock, 'I call you that because I'm used to it. You were with the French Resistance, you say? Then I suppose you learned to shoot?'

Again those cool blue eyes met hers.

'I can shoot very well. But I didn't shoot at you, Letitia Blacklock. If I *had* shot at you, I wouldn't have missed.'

Outside, there was the sound of a car driving up to the door. A few minutes later, Mitzi put her head round the door.

'It is the police again,' she said.

Craddock came in. He looked so serious that they all stared at him nervously. This was a new Inspector Craddock.

'Miss Murgatroyd has been murdered,' he said. 'She was killed – not more than an hour ago.' He looked at Julia. 'You – Miss Simmons – where have you been all day?'

'In Milchester. I've just got in.'

'And you?' said the Inspector to Patrick. 'Did you both come back together?'

'Yes – yes, we did,' said Patrick.

'No,' said Julia. 'It's no good, Patrick. That's the kind of lie that will be found out at once. The bus people know us well. I came back on the earlier bus, Inspector. I went for a walk.'

'In the direction of Boulders?'

'No. I went across the fields.'

He stared at her and Julia stared back. Before anyone could speak, the telephone rang. Miss Blacklock picked it up.

'Yes. Who? Oh, Bunch. What? No. No, she hasn't. I've no idea … Yes, he's here now.' She lowered the phone. 'Mrs Harmon would like to speak to you, Inspector. Miss Marple hasn't come back to the vicarage and Mrs Harmon is worried.'

Craddock took the telephone from Miss Blacklock. Bunch's voice was shaking like a child's.

'I'm worried, Inspector. Aunt Jane's out there somewhere – and I don't know where. And they say that Miss Murgatroyd's been killed. Is it true?'

'Yes, it's true, Mrs Harmon. Miss Marple was there with Miss Hinchcliffe when they found the body. She left there about half an hour ago. So she isn't with you?'

'No – she isn't,' said Bunch. 'I'm frightened, Inspector.'

'So am *I*,' thought Craddock. 'I'll come round to you – at once,' he said.

'Oh, *do* – there's a piece of paper. She was writing on it before she went out. I don't know if it means anything.'

Craddock put the phone down.

Miss Blacklock said anxiously, 'Has something happened to Miss Marple? Oh, I hope not. She's so old – and weak.' She stood pulling with her hand at the pearls round her neck. 'Whoever's doing this must be mad, Inspector – quite mad …'

Suddenly the choker of pearls broke under Miss Blacklock's nervous fingers. The large white pearls rolled all over the room.

'My pearls — my *pearls* — ' she cried out. The pain in her voice was so real that everyone looked at her in surprise. She turned, her hand to her throat, and rushed, crying, out of the room.

Phillipa began picking up the pearls.

'I've never seen her so upset about anything,' she said. 'Of course — she always wears them. Do you think that Randall Goedler gave them to her? They're not — *real?*'

Craddock was going to reply, 'Real? Of course not!' But then he stopped. The pearls were very large and white. They looked false — they must be false. But if they were real, they would be worth a lot of money, especially if Randall Goedler had given them to her. Would they be worth murdering someone for?

♦

Inspector Craddock went round to the vicarage, where Bunch and her husband were waiting for him with anxious faces.

'Did she say she was coming back here?' asked Bunch.

'She didn't actually say so,' said Craddock slowly. 'She was talking to Sergeant Fletcher when I last saw her. Just by the gate. And then she went through it and out. She slipped away very quietly. Fletcher may know something! Where's Fletcher?'

Craddock rang up Boulders. Then he rang up the police station in Milchester. But Fletcher wasn't at either place.

Bunch brought a piece of paper to him. He spread it out on the table. The writing was shaky and not easy to read.

'*Lamp. Violets. Where is the bottle of aspirin? Delicious death,*' Bunch read. 'That's Mitzi's cake. *Sad illness bravely suffered . . . Pearls.* And then *Lotty* – no, *Letty.* Her "e"s look like "o"s. Does it mean anything?' Bunch asked. 'Anything at all? I can't see any connection. What does she mean about pearls?'

'I don't know,' said Craddock, 'but the pearls aren't important now. We must find Miss Marple before it's too late. And where is Sergeant Fletcher?'

As Craddock left the vicarage and went back to his car, a voice spoke to him out of the wet bushes.

'Sir!' said Sergeant Fletcher. '*Sir* … '

Chapter 11   At Little Paddocks

Dinner had ended at Little Paddocks. It had been a silent and uncomfortable meal. Miss Blacklock had come downstairs again, but she had stopped trying to be cheerful. Mitzi had announced that she was frightened and that she was going to lock herself in her room. So Julia had cooked the dinner instead. Now they were in the sitting-room, with coffee on the small table by the fire. Nobody seemed to have anything to say.

At 8.30 Inspector Craddock telephoned.

'I shall be with you in about a quarter of an hour's time,' he said. 'I'm bringing Colonel and Mrs Easterbrook and Mrs Swettenham and her son with me.'

'Have you – found Miss Marple?' asked Miss Blacklock.

'No,' said the Inspector, and put down the phone.

Julia took the coffee cups back to the kitchen. To her surprise, she found Mitzi there.

'See what you have done in my nice kitchen!' said Mitzi. 'You have ruined all my pans. I only use this pan for eggs. And you, you have used it for frying onions.'

The door bell rang. Julia went to the door and opened it.

It was Miss Hinchcliffe.

'Good evening,' she said in her deep voice. 'Sorry to burst in. I expect the Inspector's telephoned?'

'He didn't tell us you were coming,' said Julia, leading the way to the sitting-room.

'He said I needn't come – but I wanted to.'

'Turn all the lights on,' said Miss Blacklock. 'And put more coal on the fire. I'm cold – horribly cold. Come and sit here by the fire, Miss Hinchcliffe.'

'Mitzi's come down again,' said Julia.

'Has she? Sometimes I think that girl's mad – quite mad.'

The sound of a car was heard outside. A few minutes later, Craddock came in with Colonel and Mrs Easterbrook and Edmund and Mrs Swettenham. They were all curiously quiet.

'Ha! A good fire,' said the Colonel. But his voice sounded thin and weak.

Mrs Easterbrook wouldn't take off her fur coat, and sat down next to her husband. Her face, usually pretty, was like the face of a little trapped rat. Edmund stared at everybody angrily. Mrs Swettenham started to talk nervously. She talked and talked.

'Mother,' said Edmund at last, 'can't you shut up?'

'Of course, dear. I don't want to say a *word*,' said Mrs Swettenham, and sat down on the sofa by Julia. Inspector Craddock stood by the door. Facing him, almost in a row, were the three women: Julia and Mrs Swettenham on the sofa, Mrs Easterbook on the arm of her husband's chair. Miss Blacklock and Miss Hinchcliffe were bending over the fire. Edmund stood near them and Phillipa was back in the shadows.

'You all know that Miss Murgatroyd's been killed,' began Craddock. 'We believe that the person who killed her was a woman. So I'm going to ask some of the ladies here to tell me what they were doing between four and twenty past four this afternoon. I've already had a statement from the young lady who has been calling herself Miss Simmons. I will ask her to repeat it.'

'I was walking along the field leading down to the river by Compton Farm,' said Julia. 'I didn't go near Boulders.'

'Mrs Swettenham?' asked the Inspector.

'Well, of course it's difficult to say – exactly –,' said Mrs Swettenham. 'I *think* I was doing some sewing. But if I *wasn't*, I was doing some gardening – no, that was earlier, before the rain.'

'The rain,' said the Inspector, 'started at 4.10 exactly.'

'Ah. It was raining so hard that water was coming through the roof. I thought the pipes outside must be blocked again with dead leaves. I called Edmund, but he didn't answer, so I went outside to clean the pipes myself. It took a long time, but I cleared out all the leaves. Then I came in and made tea.'

'Did anybody see you when you were outside?' asked Inspector Craddock.

'No,' said Mrs Swettenham. 'But you can look at the pipes. They're beautifully clean.'

'Did you hear your mother call to you, Mr Swettenham?'

'No,' said Edmund. 'I was asleep.'

'Edmund,' said his mother, 'I thought you were *writing*.'

Inspector Craddock turned to Mrs Easterbrook.

'I was sitting with Archie in his study,' said Mrs Easterbrook, fixing wide, innocent eyes on him. 'We were listening to the radio together, weren't we, Archie?'

There was a pause. Colonel Easterbrook was very red in the face. He took his wife's hand in his.

'You don't understand these things, Laura,' he said. He turned to the Inspector. 'My wife, you know, has been terribly upset by all this. She's nervous and doesn't understand the importance of – of thinking before she makes a statement.'

'Archie,' cried Mrs Easterbrook, 'are you going to say you weren't with me?'

'Well, I *wasn't* with you, my dear, was I? I was talking to Lampson, the farmer over at Croft End, about some chickens. I didn't get home until after the rain had stopped.'

'And had you been out too, Mrs Easterbrook?'

The pretty face looked even more like a small rat.

'No – no, I just sat listening to the radio. I'd been out earlier. About – about half-past three. Just for a little walk. Not far.'

'That's all, Mrs Easterbrook,' said Craddock quietly.

'Why don't you ask the others where they were?' said Mrs Easterbrook sharply. 'That Haymes woman? And Edmund Swettenham? How do you know he was asleep indoors?'

Inspector Craddock said quietly, 'Before she died, Miss Murgatroyd made a certain statement. On the night of the hold-up here, someone was absent from this room. Miss Murgatroyd told her friend the names of people she *did* see. She then discovered there was someone she did *not* see.'

'Amy was over there behind the door, where Inspector Craddock is now,' said Miss Hinchcliffe. 'She was the only person who could see anything of what was happening.'

'*Aha! That is what you think, is it!*' shouted Mitzi, as she threw open the door excitedly. 'Ah, you do not ask Mitzi to come in here with the others, do you? I am only Mitzi! Mitzi in the kitchen! Let her stay where she belongs! But I tell you that Mitzi can see things as well as anyone, and perhaps better, yes better.

'Yes, I see things. I saw something the night of the burglary. I saw something and I did not quite believe it. I think to myself I will not tell what I have seen, not yet. I will wait.'

'And when everything had calmed down, you meant to ask for a little money from a certain person, eh?' said Craddock.

Mitzi turned on him like an angry cat.

'And why not? Especially if one day there will be money – much, *much* money. Oh! I have heard things – I know about this Pippenemmer – this secret society which *she*' – she looked at Julia – 'works for. Yes, I was waiting before I asked for money – but now I am afraid. So I will tell what I know.'

'All right,' said the Inspector. 'What *do* you know?'

'I will tell you,' said Mitzi. 'On that night I am *not* in the kitchen cleaning silver as I said – I am already in the dining-room when I hear the gun. I look through the keyhole. The hall is black, but the gun goes off again and the torch falls – and it swings round as it falls – and I see her. I see her there close to him with the gun in her hand. I see Miss Blacklock.'

'Me?' Miss Blacklock sat up in surprise. 'You must be mad!'

'But that's not possible!' cried Edmund.

 Craddock interrupted with a voice as cold and sharp as a knife.

'*Isn't it, Mr Swettenham*? *And why not*? Because it *wasn't* Miss Blacklock who was standing there with the gun? It was *you*, wasn't it? *You* took Colonel Easterbrook's gun. *You* made the arrangement with Rudi Scherz. When the lights went out, you hurried through the oiled door. You shot at Miss Blacklock and then you killed Rudi Scherz. A few seconds later, you were back in the sitting-room.'

For a moment, Edmund could not speak. Then he said, 'That's a *crazy* idea. Why *me*? What motive had *I* got?'

'If Miss Blacklock dies before Mrs Goedler, two people inherit her money, remember? The two that we know of as Pip and Emma. Julia Simmons is Emma –'

'And you think I'm Pip?' Edmund laughed. 'That's *crazy*.'

'He isn't Pip.' The voice came from the shadows in the corner. Phillipa Haymes came forward, her face pale. '*I'm* Pip.'

'*You*, Mrs Haymes?'

'Yes. Everybody has been thinking that Pip was a boy – Julia knew, of course, that her twin was another girl – I don't know why she didn't say so this afternoon –'

'Family loyalty,' said Julia. 'I suddenly realised who you were. I'd had no idea until that moment.'

'I'd had the same idea as Julia,' said Phillipa, her voice shaking a little. 'After I – lost my husband and the war ended, I wondered what I was going to do. My mother died years ago. I found out about my Goedler relations. Mrs Goedler was dying, and after her death the money would go to a Miss Blacklock. I found out where Miss Blacklock lived and I – I came here. I hoped that Miss Blacklock might, perhaps, help me with Harry's education. And then,' Phillipa spoke faster, 'that hold-up happened and I began to be afraid. Because I thought that the only person with a motive for killing Miss Blacklock was me.'

She stopped and pushed her fair hair back. Craddock suddenly realised that the photograph in the box of letters was a picture of Phillipa's mother. They looked the same. He knew too why the mention of closing and unclosing hands had seemed familiar – Phillipa was doing it now.

'Miss Blacklock has been good to me,' said Phillipa. 'Very, *very* good to me – I didn't try to kill her. I never thought of killing her. But I'm Pip.' She added, 'You see, you needn't suspect Edmund any more.'

'Needn't I?' said Craddock. 'Edmund Swettenham's a young man, perhaps, who would like to marry a rich wife. But she wouldn't be a rich wife *unless Miss Blacklock died before Mrs Goedler*. So he had to make sure that happened – *didn't you, Mr Swettenham?*'

'It's a lie!' Edmund shouted.

And then, suddenly, a sound was heard from the kitchen – a long, high scream of terror.

'That isn't Mitzi!' cried Julia.

'No,' said Inspector Craddock, 'it's the murderer … '

♦

When the Inspector had started shouting at Edmund Swettenham, Mitzi had left the sitting-room quietly and gone back to the kitchen. She was running water into the sink when Miss Blacklock entered.

'What a liar you are, Mitzi,' said Miss Blacklock. 'And that isn't the way to wash up. Wash the silver first, and fill the sink right up. You haven't got enough water in there.'

Mitzi turned the taps on obediently.

'You are not angry at what I say, Miss Blacklock?' she asked. 'Shall I go and say to the Inspector that I made it all up?'

'He knows that already,' said Miss Blacklock pleasantly.

Mitzi turned off the taps. As she did so, two hands came up behind her head and forced it down into the sink. Mitzi fought and struggled, but Miss Blacklock was strong and her hands held the girl's head firmly under water.

Then, from somewhere quite close behind her, Dora Bunner's voice rose up: '*Oh, Lotty – Lotty – don't do it … Lotty.*'

Miss Blacklock screamed. Her hands flew up in the air, and Mitzi's head came up out of the water. Miss Blacklock screamed again and again – because there was no one else in the kitchen.

'*Dora, Dora, forgive me. I had to … I had to –*'

She rushed towards the door. Suddenly Sergeant Fletcher stepped out of the cupboard where the brushes were kept. Miss Marple stepped out behind him.

'I'm very good at imitating people's voices,' said Miss Marple.

'I witnessed your attempt to drown this girl, madam,' said Sergeant Fletcher. 'I must warn you, Letitia Blacklock –'

'*Charlotte* Blacklock,' corrected Miss Marple. 'That's who she is, you know. Under that choker of pearls she always wears, you'll find the mark left by the operation.'

'Operation?'

'Operation for goitre. I've known about it for some time.'

Charlotte Blacklock sat down by the table and began to cry.

'Why did you do that?' she said. 'Make Dora's voice come? I loved Dora. I really loved Dora.'

Inspector Craddock and the others had crowded in the doorway.

As soon as Mitzi could speak, she started to praise herself.

'I did that well, didn't I?' she said. 'I am clever! I am brave! Oh, I am brave! *I* was nearly murdered too.'

Miss Hinchcliffe rushed towards Charlotte Blacklock, but Sergeant Fletcher held her back.

'No – no, Miss Hinchcliffe –'

'Let me get at her,' Miss Hinchcliffe was saying. 'Just let me get at her. She killed Amy Murgatroyd.'

Charlotte Blacklock looked up.

'I didn't want to kill her. I didn't want to kill anybody – I had to – but it's Dora I care about – oh, Dora, Dora –'

And once again she dropped her head on her hands and cried.

Chapter 12   Evening at the Vicarage

Miss Marple sat in the tall armchair at the vicarage. Bunch was on the floor in front of the fire with her arms around her knees. Reverend Julian Harmon was there too. Inspector Craddock was enjoying a drink and looking very relaxed. Julia, Patrick, Edmund and Phillipa were also in the room.

'When did you first think that Miss Blacklock had arranged the hold-up, Aunt Jane?' asked Bunch.

'Well, at the beginning, I was deceived like everyone else. I thought that someone really did want to kill Letitia Blacklock.'

'Did that Swiss boy recognise her?' asked Bunch.

'Yes. He'd worked in Dr Adolf Koch's private hospital in Berne,' said Craddock. 'Koch was a world-famous specialist in operations for goitre. Charlotte Blacklock went there to have her goitre removed and Rudi Scherz was one of the attendants. When he came to England, he recognised her in the hotel as a lady who had been a patient. He decided to speak to her.'

'So his father didn't own a hotel in Montreux?'

'Oh, no, she made that up to explain why he spoke to her.'

'It was probably a great shock to her,' said Miss Marple, thoughtfully. 'She felt safe – and then – someone arrived who had known her definitely as *Charlotte* Blacklock.

'But the story started when Charlotte – a pretty, affectionate girl – developed goitre. It ruined her life, because she was a very sensitive girl. As her goitre grew larger and uglier, she became very depressed. She shut herself up and refused to see people. Letitia loved her sister. She was worried by Charlotte's depression. When the girls' father died, Letitia gave up her job with Randall

Goedler. She took Charlotte to Switzerland, where Charlotte had an operation to remove the goitre. The operation was successful. It had left a mark, but this was easily hidden by a choker of pearls. By this time, the war had started. It was difficult for the sisters to return to England, so they stayed in Switzerland. Occasionally they received news from England. They learned that Belle Goedler could not live long. They probably talked about what they would do after Letitia had inherited Belle's money. Charlotte would be free at last to enjoy life – to travel, and to have a beautiful house.

'But suddenly Letitia became ill and died. And all Charlotte's dreams died with her. She had lost her sister, but she had also lost the chance of a lot of money. Then she had an idea. The money was meant to come to Letitia. Why shouldn't Charlotte pretend that *Charlotte* had died and *Letitia* was alive? She bought a house in a part of England that was quite unknown to her. Everyone knew her as Letitia Blacklock. It was really very easy because so few people had ever really known Charlotte.

'She settled down at Little Paddocks and met her neighbours. Then she got a letter from her two young cousins, asking dear Letitia if they could come and stay with her. She accepted with pleasure the visit of two young cousins she had never seen. And they accepted her as Aunt Letty. Everything was going well. And then – she made a big mistake. She got a letter from Dora Bunner, an old school friend. She had been really fond of Dora, because Dora reminded her of her happy schooldays. So she went to see her. Dora was, no doubt, very surprised! She'd written to *Letitia* and the sister who came to see her was *Charlotte.* Charlotte told Dora what she had done. And Dora thought it was absolutely right that dear Lotty should receive the money that was meant for Letty. Lotty had suffered bravely and patiently for a long time, and now she *deserved* a reward.

'So Dora came to live at Little Paddocks – and very soon Charlotte began to understand that she had made a terrible mistake. Dora was often confused. Sometimes by mistake she called Charlotte "Lotty" instead of "Letty". Then something worse happened. Charlotte was recognised and spoken to by Rudi Scherz at the Royal Spa Hotel. She became very worried about him. Perhaps he would tell everyone that she was not Letitia. So she decided to kill him.

'She told Rudi Scherz that she wanted to arrange a joke "hold-up" at a party. She paid him well to act the part of the robber. She gave him the advertisement to put in the paper, and arranged for him to visit the house. She took Colonel Easterbrook's gun out of his drawer when she was visiting his house. She oiled the door in the sitting-room so that it would open and shut noiselessly. It probably seemed like a game. But it wasn't.

'She went out just after six to "shut up the hens". She let Scherz into the house then, and gave him the mask and gloves and the torch. At 6.30 she was ready by the small table, with her hand on the cigarette-box. When the clock began to strike, everyone looked at it. Only one person, Dora, kept looking at Miss Blacklock. And she told us, in her first statement, exactly what Miss Blacklock had done. She'd picked up the vase of violets. She'd previously cut the flex of the lamp so it was almost cut through. She picked up the violets, spilled the water and switched on the lamp. Everything fused and the lights went out.'

'Just like the other afternoon at the vicarage,' said Bunch.

'Yes, my dear. And I was puzzled about those lights. I'd realised that there were two lamps, a pair, and that one had been changed for the other – probably during the night.'

'That's right,' said Craddock. 'When Fletcher examined the lamp the next morning, it was fine – the flex wasn't frayed.'

'I'd understood what Dora Bunner meant by saying it had been the shepherdess the night before,' said Miss Marple, 'but I had thought at first that Patrick was responsible. But Dora Bunner saw Letitia pick up the violets –'

'And she saw what she described as a flash and a bang,' interrupted Craddock.

82

'And, of course, when dear Bunch spilled the water on to the flex here – I realised at once that it was Miss Blacklock who fused the lights because only she was near that table.'

'And the violets died because there was no water in the vase,' said Craddock. 'That was a mistake – she forgot to fill it up again. But I suppose she thought nobody would notice. As soon as the lights went out, she went out through the oiled door and behind Scherz. She had put on her gardening gloves and had the gun in her hand. She fired quickly twice and then, as he swung round, she held the gun close to his body and shot him. She dropped the gun, then went back into the sitting-room. She cut her ear – I don't quite know how –'

'Nail scissors, I expect,' said Miss Marple. 'Just a small cut on the ear lets out a lot of blood. That was very good psychology, of course. The blood running down over her white blouse made it seem certain that she *had* been shot at.

'After the discovery of the oiled door, we started to look for someone with a motive to kill Letitia Blacklock. And there was someone with a motive, and Miss Blacklock knew it. Phillipa. I think she recognised Phillipa almost at once. She had seen pictures of her mother, Sonia Goedler. Strangely, Charlotte became very fond of Phillipa. She told herself that when she inherited the money, Phillipa and Harry could live with her. But when the Inspector found out about "Pip and Emma", Charlotte became worried. She didn't want anyone to suspect Phillipa. She tried her best to protect her. She told you that Sonia was small and dark and she hid the photos of Sonia.

'But it was Dora Bunner who was the real danger,' Miss Marple continued. 'Every day, Dora became more forgetful and talked more. Sometimes she called Miss Blacklock "Lotty".

'The day we had coffee in the Bluebird Café, I had the odd impression that Dora was talking about two people, not one – and, of course, she was. At one moment she spoke of her friend as not being pretty, but then she said she was pretty and light-hearted. I think Charlotte heard a lot of that conversation when she came into

83

the café that morning. Charlotte realised that life could not be safe for her while Dora Bunner was alive. She loved Dora – she didn't want to kill her – but she couldn't see any other way. The strange thing was that she did her best to make Bunny's last day a happy one. The birthday party – and the special cake …'

'Delicious Death,' said Patrick.

'Yes – yes – it was rather like that … She tried to give her friend a delicious death – the party, and all the things she liked to eat. And then the pills in the aspirin bottle by her bed, so Bunny would go there to get some. And it would seem, as it did seem, that the pills had been meant for *Letitia* …

'And so Bunny died in her sleep, quite happily, and Charlotte felt safe again. But she missed Dora Bunner – she missed her sweetness and her loyalty, she missed talking to her about the old days … She cried the day I came here with a note from Julian – and her tears were real. She'd killed her own dear friend.'

'That's horrible,' said Bunch. 'Horrible.'

'But it's very human,' said Julian Harmon. 'One forgets how human murderers are.'

'I know,' said Miss Marple. 'Human. But very dangerous too. Poor Miss Murgatroyd. Charlotte probably arrived at the cottage and heard Miss Hinchcliffe and Miss Murgatroyd acting out the murder. It was a great shock to her. As Miss Hinchcliffe rushed to the station, Miss Murgatroyd called after her, "She wasn't there …" I asked Miss Hinchcliffe if that was the way she said it. If she had said, "*She* wasn't there," that would have meant she was thinking about a person – "*That's* the one. *She* wasn't *there*." But it was a place that was in her mind – a place where she expected someone to be – but there wasn't anybody there. "How extraordinary, Hinch," Miss Murgatroyd said. "She wasn't there …" So that could only mean Letitia Blacklock …'

'But you knew before that, didn't you?' said Bunch. 'When the lamp fused. When you wrote down those things on the paper.'

'Yes. The different parts came together – and made a pattern.'

'*Lamp*. Yes. *Violets*. Yes,' said Bunch. '*Bottle of aspirin*. You meant that Bunny had been going to buy a new bottle that day. So why did she need to take aspirins from Letitia's bottle? And then *Delicious Death*. The cake – but more than the cake. The whole party. A happy day for Bunny before she died.'

'Charlotte Blacklock was a kind woman,' said Miss Marple. 'When she said in the kitchen, "I didn't want to kill anybody," it was true. But she wanted money that didn't belong to her.'

'What made you think that Charlotte had had goitre?' asked Bunch.

'Switzerland, you know. The people who know most about goitre and the world's best specialists are Swiss. And those pearls that Letitia Blacklock always wore round her neck weren't her *style* – but they were perfect for hiding the mark from her operation.'

'I understand now why she was so upset when the string broke,' said Craddock. 'I thought it was very strange at the time.'

And after that, it was *Lotty* you wrote, not *Letty*,' said Bunch.

'Yes. I remembered that the sister's name was Charlotte, and that Dora had called Miss Blacklock "Lotty" once or twice – and that each time, she had been very upset. It all made a pattern. I went out to cool my head a little and see how I could prove everything. Then we found Miss Murgatroyd …'

Miss Marple's voice dropped. It became quiet and firm.

'I knew then something had got to be done. Quickly! But there still wasn't any *proof*. I thought out a possible plan and I talked to Sergeant Fletcher. He didn't like it, but I persuaded him. We went up to Little Paddocks, and I talked to Mitzi.

'I told her stories about girls in the Resistance. I said I could see that she was brave, and had the right sort of personality for this type of work. She got really excited. Then I persuaded her to play her part. She had to pretend that she *had* looked through the dining-room keyhole, and seen Miss Blacklock with a gun.'

'Then *I* pretended that I didn't believe her,' said the Inspector. 'I pretended to accuse Edmund –'

'And I played my part too,' said Edmund. 'I denied everything. But then you spoke, Phillipa, my love. That was a great surprise. Neither the Inspector nor I had known you were "Pip".'

'We made Charlotte Blacklock believe that Mitzi was the only person who suspected the truth,' said Miss Marple. 'Mitzi went straight back to the kitchen – as I'd told her to. Miss Blacklock came after her almost immediately. She didn't know that Sergeant Fletcher and I were hiding in the cupboard.'

'But why were you in the cupboard too, Aunt Jane? Couldn't Sergeant Fletcher take care of everything himself?'

'It was safer with two of us. And I could imitate Dora Bunner's voice. If anything could break Charlotte down, that would.'

There was a long silence.

Then Julia said, 'Mitzi told me yesterday that she's taking a new job near Southampton. She is going to tell everyone how she helped the police catch a very dangerous criminal.'

'I'm sure Mitzi will soon be telling everyone how she helped the police with not one, but hundreds of cases!' said Edmund.

♦

Phillipa and Edmund got married. Soon after their wedding, they went to the newspaper shop.

'What papers would you like to order, sir?' asked Mr Totman, the owner of the shop.

'*The Daily Worker,*' said Edmund firmly.

'And the *Daily Telegraph*,' said Phillipa. 'And *Gardener's World*.'

'Thank you, sir,' said Mr Totman. 'And the *Gazette*?'

'*No,*' said Phillipa and Edmund together.

ACTIVITIES

Before you read

1   *A Murder Is Announced* is a detective story. What famous detectives do you know from literature, films or TV? Discuss them with another student.

   a   What do they look like?

   b   Where do they work?

   c   What makes them interesting?

2   Look at the Word List at the back of the book. Check the meanings of unfamiliar words. Then choose the most suitable word from the pair in *italics* in each of these sentences.

   a   The old lady was wearing a beautiful *goitre/choker* around her neck.

   b   The *pearls/violets* in that vase are a lovely colour of purple.

   c   Mary *glanced/sighed* quickly across the room and saw John.

   d   The plastic around the *fuse/flex* protects the electrical wire inside.

   e   Let's go into the garden after lunch and sit in the new *cottage/summerhouse*.

   f   After many years in the army, he became a *constable/colonel*.

   g   I've got a terrible headache. I'll take some *aspirin/sherry* and go to bed.

   h   He's worked as a *reverend/shepherd* all his life. He loves being outside with the sheep.

   i   After his aunt died, the contents of her *will/case* surprised everyone.

   j   The criminal's *motive/mask* for the crime remains a mystery. Nobody knows why he did it.

While you read

3   Match the people with the descriptions below. Write their names.

87

Edmund Swettenham	Mitzi
Colonel Easterbrook	Dora Bunner
Patrick Simmons	Phillipa Haymes
Mrs Harmon	Detective-Inspector Craddock
Miss Blacklock	Rudi Scherz

a Has a much younger wife. ....

b Lives at the vicarage. ....

c Works as a cook. ....

d Reads the *Daily Worker*. ....

e Asked an old school friend for help. ....

f Is in charge of a murder case. ....

g Wears a pearl choker. ....

h Has a son, away at school. ....

i Worked at the Royal Spa Hotel. ....

j Has a sister called Julia. ....

After you read

4 Talk about these people. Discuss:

a what he or she looks like

b who he or she lives with

c why he or she is at the 'party'

Miss Blacklock	Mitzi
Colonel Easterbrook	Amy Murgatroyd

5 Discuss the connections between these pairs.

a the *Chipping Cleghorn Gazette*/an invitation

b Mitzi/the Nazis

c roses/the central heating

d a vase of violets/a cigarette-box

e Phillipa Haymes/gardening

f Rudi Scherz/Myrna Harris

Chapters 4–6

Before you read

6 Imagine that you are Detective-Inspector Craddock. You are going to interview some more people about the shooting at Little Paddocks.

   a Who will you choose to interview?

   b What questions will you ask them?

While you read

7 What is Inspector Craddock told? Write short answers.

   a (by Julia) Did Rudi Scherz intend to fire at Miss Blacklock?

   ....

   b (by Mitzi) Where was Mitzi during the shootings?

   ....

   c (by Patrick Simmons) Why did Miss Blacklock open a new bottle of sherry?

   ....

   d (by Phillipa Haymes) Why was Phillipa surprised by the party?

   ....

   e (by Edmund Swettenham) Was the dining-room door really locked?

   ....

   f (by Colonel Easterbrook) Who killed Rudi Scherz?

   ....

   g (by Miss Murgatroyd) Where was she when the door opened?

   ....

   h (by Mrs Harmon) What did she see during the shooting?

   ....

8 What do the police learn from Miss Marple? Circle the wrong words in each sentence, and write the correct ones.

   a She has written a letter to Sir Henry from the Royal Spa Hotel   ....

   b Rudi Scherz signed one of her cheques.   ....

   c Myrna Harris is behaving normally at work.   ....

   d Rudi Scherz was paid to fire the gun.   ....

9 Complete these sentences.

    a Mitzi believes that Rudi Scherz was working with ....

    ....

    b Dora Bunner is surprised that the second door to the
sitting-room ....

    c Inspector Craddock thinks that when Rudi Scherz arrived
in the house, the murderer was ....

10 Inspector Craddock makes notes during his interview with
Miss Blacklock. Match the names with the information.

    a Patrick and Julia   **1)** married Randall Goedler's sister.

    b Randall Goedler   **2)** quarrelled with Randall Goedler.

    c Miss Blacklock   **3)** will inherit Miss Blacklock's money.

    d Belle Goedler   **4)** helped Randall Goedler become rich.

    e Pip and Emma   **5)** is seriously ill.

    f Sonia   **6)** are Randall Goedler's relatives.

    g Dmitri Stamfordis   **7)** was a well-known businessman.

11 Which of the people in Activity 10 does Inspector Craddock
think:

    a may have a strong motive for murder? ....

    b might be in danger?   ....

After you read

12 Explain why these are important to the story.

    a a powerful torch

    b a conversation in a summerhouse

    c a door with an oiled lock

    d a will made by a rich businessman

    e an old lady living in Scotland

13 How do these people feel? Give possible reasons for their
feelings.

    a Mitzi, about Phillipa Haymes

    b Sir Henry Clithering, about Miss Marple

    c Inspector Craddock, about Mitzi

    d Miss Blacklock, about Dora Bunner

    e Inspector Craddock, about Miss Marple

Chapters 7–9

Before you read

14 Discuss the people who live in Chipping Cleghorn. Give
reasons for your answers.

    a Which ones do you think are telling the truth about
themselves?

    b Which ones might be pretending to be other people?

    c Who might get murdered next?

15 Inspector Craddock is planning to travel to Scotland.

    a Who is he going to see there?

    b What questions might he plan to ask?

While you read

16 Miss Marple talks to Mrs Harmon about people she has
known in the past. Which people in Chipping Cleghorn do
they remind her of? Write the names.

    a Nurse Ellerton   ....

    b Mrs Pusey's nephew   ....

    c Mrs Cray   ....

    d the girl at St Jean de Collines   ....

    e Mr Hodgson   ....

17 Which of these people is present at Dora Bunner's birthday
party? Circle Yes or No.

    a Miss Marple   YES / NO

    b Patrick Simmons   YES / NO

    c Miss Blacklock   YES / NO

    d Mrs Harmon   YES / NO

    e Mrs Easterbrook   YES / NO

    f Julia Simmons   YES / NO

    g Inspector Craddock   YES / NO

    h Miss Hinchcliffe   YES / NO

    i Phillipa Haymes   YES / NO

    j Edmund Swettenham   YES / NO

After you read

18 Why are these people surprised (or why do they seem
surprised) about these things?

    a Sergeant Fletcher/Mrs Swettenham's visit to Little
Paddocks

   b Miss Hinchcliffe/the door at Little Paddocks

   c Colonel Easterbrook/a gun

   d Dora Bunner/two lamps

   e Phillipa Haymes/Miss Blacklock's will

   f Miss Blacklock and Julia/a book of photographs

   g Amy Murgatroyd/her sudden memory of the night of Scherz's death

19 Discuss possible reasons for Dora Bunner's murder. Who do you think is the most likely murderer?

20 Discuss whether the following statements are true or false according to the information in the story.

   a Pip and Emma are in Chipping Cleghorn.

   b Belle Goedler will live longer than Miss Blacklock.

   c Someone put poison into Mitzi's cake.

   d Phillipa Haymes met Rudi Scherz in the summerhouse.

   e Miss Blacklock hasn't seen Sonia for many years.

   f Amy Murgatroyd knows who killed Rudi Scherz.

21 Discuss these questions.

   a 'There isn't very much time.' What does Miss Marple mean? Why is she worried?

   b Why was Captain Haymes definitely not the killer?

   c How does a cat help Miss Marple solve a problem?

   d What was special about Miss Murgatroyd's position in the sitting-room on the night of the hold-up?

Chapters 10–12

Before you read

22 Discuss these questions.

   a Who do you think Miss Murgatroyd was talking about when she said, 'She wasn't there'?

   b What do you think may happen to Miss Murgatroyd now?

23 Which of these people do you think could be Sonia Goedler, or a relative of Sonia Goedler? Discuss your reasons.

   a Patrick and Julia Simmons

   b Mrs Easterbrook

   c Mrs Swettenham

   d Phillipa Haymes

While you read

24 In which order do these events happen in this part of the
story? Number them 1–8.

   a Mitzi is attacked. ......

   b A wedding takes place. ......

   c Miss Blacklock receives a letter. ......

   d Someone is murdered. ......

   e A pearl choker breaks. ......

   f Miss Marple explains. ......

   g People arrive at Little Paddocks. ......

   h The murderer is caught. ......

After you read

25 Complete the table. What do these people say that they were
doing between 4.00 and 4.20 in the afternoon of the day
when the third murder took place?

Julia Simmons	
Mrs Swettenham	
Edmund Swettenham	
Colonel Easterbrook	
Mrs Easterbrook	

26 Work with a partner. Discuss the connections between these
people and things.

   a Julia Simmons/a theatre company

   b Miss Marple/a cupboard of brushes

   c Miss Blacklock/nail scissors

   d Mitzi/the French Resistance

   e Switzerland/goitre

   f Rudi Scherz/a hospital in Berne

27 Which of these people has a secret to hide from other people
in the story? What is their secret, or what might it be?

   a Miss Blacklock

b Patrick Simmons

c Julia Simmons

d Mrs Harmon

e Mrs Easterbrook

f Phillipa Haymes

g Mrs Swettenham

h Miss Hinchcliffe

28 Explain how the list in Miss Marple's notebook helps her discover who the murderer is.

a Lamp

b Violets

c Delicious Death

d Sad illness bravely suffered

e Pearls

f Letty/Lotty

29 Complete the table with information about the three murders.

	Name of murdered person	Method	Reason for murder
First murder			
Second murder			
Third murder			

30 Some things are not made clear in the story. Discuss possible explanations.

a How and when did the murderer get Colonel Easterbrook's gun?

b What happened to the gun after Rudi Scherz was shot?

c Why did Mrs Easterbrook lie to Inspector Craddock when he asked her where she was on the afternoon of the third murder?

Writing

31 You have something unusual that you want to buy or sell. You decide to advertise it in the Personal Column of the *Chipping Cleghorn Gazette*. Write your advertisement.

32 Write Dora Bunner's letter to 'Letitia' Blacklock. Introduce yourself as her old schoolfriend, and ask if she remembers you. Say that you are unwell and have very little money. Ask her to help you.

33 Imagine that you are Mrs Harmon and that you have a private diary. Write about what happened on the evening of Rudi Scherz's murder at Little Paddocks. Write about the events and your own feelings.

34 Mitzi has a cookery book. Write the instructions for making the chocolate cake that Patrick calls 'Delicious Death'.

35 Imagine that you are Inspector Craddock. Choose three of the people that you interview after the first murder and write notes about them.

36 Write a letter from Phillipa Haymes's husband, Captain Ronald Haymes, to Phillipa, asking for money. Explain that you have run away from the army and are in trouble. Ask for Phillipa's help.

37 Write the report that the Swiss police send to Chief Constable Rydesdale about Rudi Scherz. Include a list of Scherz's crimes and say how much time he has spent in prison.

38 Imagine that you are Miss Marple. You want to persuade Mitzi to help you catch the murderer. Tell her about the girls in the French Resistance and persuade her to act out a part. Write your conversation.

39 It is a year after the story ends. Imagine that you are Phillipa Haymes. Write to your sister Emma, inviting her to your wedding.

40 Write a reader's report on *A Murder Is Announced*. Introduce the plot (without giving the ending) and the characters, and explain why you think the book is (or isn't) a successful detective story.

WORD LIST

aspirin (n) a medicine that reduces pain

attic (n) a space or a room just below the roof of a house

candle (n) a stick of wax which you burn to give light

case (n) an event, or a number of events, that police or detectives are trying to learn more about

choker (n) a piece of jewellery that fits tightly around a woman's neck

colonel (n) an officer with a high position in the army

column (n) short lines of writing arranged below each other on a newspaper page

constable (n) an officer with a low position in the British police. The **Chief Constable** is the officer in charge of the police in a large area of Britain.

cottage (n) a small house, usually in the country or a village

deliberate (adj) intended or planned

flex (n) an electrical wire covered with plastic

fray (v) to become damaged at the edge. If an old piece of cloth or a rope frays, pieces become loose and it starts to come apart.

fuse (n/v) a short, thin piece of wire that stops electricity reaching and damaging electrical equipment when too much power runs through it

glance (v) to look quickly at someone or something

goitre (n) a large swelling on the front part of the neck

hold-up (n; hold up, v) an attempt to rob someone by threatening them with a weapon

inherit (v) to receive money or property from someone after they have died

invalid (n) someone who needs to be looked after as a result of illness, old age or an accident

mask (n/v) something that you wear to hide all or part of your face

motive (n) the reason why someone does something

pearl (n) a valuable small, white, round object used in jewellery. Pearls are found in a type of shellfish

reverend (n) a minister of a Christian church